The United States as a Confederation and the relevance of the Tenth Amendment

by Rick M. Montes

The United States as a Confederation and the relevance of the Tenth Amendment

by Rick M. Montes
Tenth Amendment Center
Carmel, New York 10512

Rick.Montes@TenthAmendmentCenter.com

First Edition, published July 2011
Copyright © 2011 by Rick M. Montes

ISBN 4-87187-903-8
978-4-87187-903-3

Ishi Press International
1664 Davidson Avenue, Suite 1B
Bronx NY 10453-7877
USA
1-917-507-7226

Printed in the United States of America

Acknowledgment

I would like to give thanks to Dr. Kevin R.C. Gutzman, Constitutional Scholar and Defender of Liberty, for allowing me the opportunity to complete this paper for my Thesis as a Graduate Student at Western Connecticut State University.

Deo Vindice

<u>Table of Contents</u>:

The United States as a Confederation and the relevance of the Tenth Amendment

Today if you asked the average citizen of any of the fifty States: "Which has ultimate jurisdiction, the Federal government or the individual States?" the answer would likely be "The Federal government." If you were to ask this same question to either a Federal or State Attorney or Judge, you would in all likelihood receive the same answer. With so many people believing this to be true, especially professionals who make their living having the responsibility of knowing the answer, why should anyone doubt the validity of the Federal government's supremacy over the States? Why does it even matter?

Throughout our Republic we are witnessing a phenomenon called the "Tea Party." This Tea Party consists of hundreds of thousands of citizens upset with the expansive growth of the Federal government. They seek to rein in government spending, stop judicial activism, and return, as a recent Newsweek.com article stated, "A Constitutional fundamentalism that would limit the federal government to the exercise of enumerated powers" (Weisberg 2010). Opponents criticize these same citizens as "Right Wing" and "Racist." On the official website of The Communist Party USA, an essay was posted entitled: "Hope is stronger than hate" which stated, "In their efforts to win back Congress… Tea Party attack dogs are unashamedly promoting fear, racism, bigotry and red baiting." (Tyner 2010)

The debate centers on the proper role of government, with passions high on both sides. Many Conservatives and Tea Party activists are lamenting that our Constitution is being subverted and destroyed by the "Left" and the Socialist. Yet, these same "less government" adherents seek involvement by the Federal government in a myriad of matters which include, The War on Drugs, the definition of marriage as one man and one woman, prohibiting abortion, allowing school prayer and protecting the right to keep and bear firearms. Their opponents agree that the Federal government should be involved but for completely different reasons. Those on the so-called "left" wish the Federal government to act by severely restricting firearms, allowing abortion, denying the rights of students to say a prayer at school and allowing homosexual marriage. Both groups feel it is necessary for the Federal government to be involved. Who is right?

If we are to have an educated discussion on these issues, we must understand the Constitutional role of our government and the proper relationship between Federal and State authority. The answer to the above question, which one has ultimate authority, The Federal or State governments, is the core to that understanding. It is only when we become aware that it was the States who created the Federal government and that the created cannot be supreme to the creator, can we begin to have that discussion.

So what does all of this have to do with the topic of this paper? Let me explain. We the people of these united States are very diverse. We come from different backgrounds and ethnic groups. Some like the warm weather of the South and some the snowy winters of the North. Some of us like the wide-open plains of the central States and some like the majestic mountains of the Pacific North West. We are an individualistic people with differing opinions on everything from the definition of marriage, to gun laws and abortion, welfare and religion. I believe this is what makes us such a great people and allowed us collectively to become the greatest nation on Earth. It is what makes us unique. It is precisely this diversity and uniqueness that many of our Founding Fathers counted on when, on a hot day in July, 1776, thirteen separate colonies declared their independence to the world. This is the story of those thirteen, individual and dissimilar colonies, made up of a conglomeration of people seeking the freedom to live their lives as they saw fit. It is a story that needs to be told because, unfortunately, many people today do not understand that their freedom as a diverse people is vanishing. We have gone from local management and administration in our home States, Counties and Towns to a people controlled by a faceless, all encompassing, parasitic entity called the Federal government. Sadly, most people just do not understand the true relationship between the States and the Federal Government, especially those who should, such as Attorneys and "Constitutional Scholars." They forget about the uniqueness that makes us who we are.

Therefore, the purpose of this paper is to show the relationship between the States and the Federal government, not only as it was intended by those who created the current Constitution and the people of the States who ratified it, but by understanding the reason why people came to America in the first place, who they looked to for guidance when creating their governments, what the Declaration of Independence meant to the people of that day and why these same States created our first Constitution, the Articles of Confederation. I will show by historical documentation, with heavy reliance on their own words that the delegates to the Federal

Convention and the people of the individual States debated the issue of having a National government, with its idea of a supreme legislature, judiciary and executive, or a Republic, with its limited and enumerated powers, quite thoroughly. In fact, during the first few days of the Convention, a resolution was brought forth by Edmund Randolph of Virginia, a man of high stature during the course of the proceedings, that read: "That a union of the States merely federal will not accomplish the object proposed by the Articles of Confederation, namely "common defense", security of liberty, and general welfare"... that therefore a national government ought to be established consisting of a supreme legislature, judiciary and executive." A delegate from South Carolina, Mr. Charles Pinckney, "wished to know whether the establishment of this Resolution is intended as a ground for a consolidation of the several States into one" (Farrand, The Records of the Federal Convention of 1787 v.I, 40-41). Mr. Randolph's reply to that inquiry is the crux of the entire debate, he stated: "...It is only meant to give the national government a power to defend and protect itself. *To take therefore from the respective legislatures or States, no more sovereignty than is competent to this end*" (Farrand, The Records of the Federal Convention of 1787 v.I, 42)

That these United States are a confederation of sovereign entities, made up of people who were jealous of their freedom, who fought a war and declared Independence to remain free from an all powerful, centralized government, and created a government for their mutual "defense, safety and general welfare, will become apparent. It is only if we understand why the people of the States decided to unite and create a Constitution in the first place can we hope to save it, or some may say, resuscitate it.

Freedom

Nearly four hundred years ago individuals and families left the Old World to settle on the shores of America in search of freedom. They came not knowing what the future held for them. However, they risked their lives to build a better future for themselves and their posterity. In their decision to leave their homes and travel thousands of miles, the first settlers created new communities and societies and eventually became a distinct people within those societies who shared a common language, goals and values. In these new communities, the people began to create rules and regulations, to combine themselves together and to erect and set up such government that would be to their best "discerning, agreeable to the will of God...and to establish laws that shall upon good grounds, be made and enacted amongst them... that they may live quietly and peaceably together, in all godliness and honesty" (Lutz, 4). This is clearly shown by some of the earliest founding documents. When discussing these documents, Donald S. Lutz, a Professor of Political Science at the University of Houston, wrote: "There are four distinct foundational elements... (1) The founding or creation of a people; (2) the founding or creation of a government; (3) the self-definition of the people in shared values and goals so that the founded people may cross generations; and (4) the specification of a form of government through the creation of institutions for collective decision making" and any document can contain one, all or a combination of the four elements (Lutz, xxiii). These early settlers came for varied reasons, and in the process became distinct peoples who set up governments that reflected their uniqueness. The most important aspect of these governments was that they were formed by the consent of the people.

On May 13, 1607 the first English settlement in the New World was established at Jamestown in what would later become Virginia. These settlers came with a grant from the Crown to establish a colony, but most importantly, to make money, ultimately by growing and selling tobacco. After a few abortive attempts, suffering hardship and death, these hearty souls eventually established a permanent colony. Since most of these settlers were of English descent, they came with the knowledge of English government and its inherent rights. On May 30, 1619 the first Legislative assembly in America was formed. In this assembly the first acts of resistance to legislation without representation appeared when the Virginia assembly insisted on approving acts of the London Company, which was the initiator of the colony's charter (Fleming, 53). The Assembly session lasted only five days, but its members were considered "business-like and conservative" and had little trouble in passing legislation that was best suited for their new colony (Fleming, 56).

In November of the year 1620, in what is considered the oldest surviving compact based on popular consent, the "Mayflower Compact" [1] was signed by the inhabitants of the new Plymouth Colony. It stated their reason for their arrival and noted the formation of a Civil Body: "In the name of God, Amen. We the under-written, the Loyal Subjects of our dread Sovereign Lord King James...having undertaken for the glory of God, and advancement of the Christian Faith...a voyage to plant the first Colony in the Northern parts of

---

1 Also known as "The Plymouth Combination" it was originally known by the Plymouth inhabitants as "The Combination" and was not known as the "Mayflower Compact" until 1793 when it was reprinted outside Massachusetts for the first time. (Lutz, 31)

Virginia; Do by these Presents, solemnly and mutually, in the presence of God and one another, Covenant and *Combine ourselves together into a Civil Body Politick,* for our better ordering and preservation and furtherance of the ends aforesaid: *and by virtue hereof do enact, constitute, and frame, such just and equal Laws, Ordinances, Acts, Constitutions , and Officers, from time to time, as shall be thought most meet and convenient for the general good of the Colony..."* (Lutz, 32 emphasis added). Here we see a people, starting fresh in a new world, void of any creature comforts, realizing that some form of government should be established for the "general good of the Colony."

On July 5, 1639, nearly 137 years before the Declaration of Independence, another group of settlers felt it necessary to put in writing what they were attempting to accomplish. They wrote what would be called the "Agreement of the Settlers at Exeter in New Hampshire" and in it contained these words: *"Whereas it hath pleased the Lord to move the heart of our ...Dread Sovereign Charles...King of England...to grant license and liberty to sundry of his subjects to plant themselves in the western part's of America: We, his loyal subjects, brethren of the Church of Exeter...with other inhabitants there, considering with ourselves the holy will of god and our own necessity, that we should not live without wholesome law's & government amongst us...do in the name of Christ & in the sight of God combine ourselves together, to erect & set up amongst us such government as shall be to our best discerning, agreeable to the will of god, professing ourselves subjects to our Sovereign Lord King Charles, according to the liberties of our English Colony of the Massachusetts...submit ourselves to such godly & Christian laws as are established in the realm of England to our best knowledge & to all other such laws which shall upon good grounds, be made and enacted amongst us according to God, yet we may live quietly & peaceably together, in all godliness and honest"* (Lutz, 3-4; emphasis added). Here the new inhabitants were "declaring" that they were "planting" themselves in America and forming a government of their own consent. These were clearly a religious people and while acknowledging the benevolence of their "Dread Sovereign Charles", they also understood that their true King was the "Most High God" and their ultimate allegiance was to him. They came to the New World to seek religious freedom, build a society and enact laws of their own choosing as long as it obeyed the word of God. The "Agreement" also included an oath that each person of the community was to partake. The words contained within the oath show the autonomy of the people: *"We do swear by the Great and Dreadful name of the Most High God, Maker and Governor of heaven and earth, and by the Lord Jesus Christ, the King and Savior of his people, that in his name and fear, we will submit ourselves to be ruled and governed according to the will and word of God, and such wholesome laws and ordinances as shall be derived therefrom by our honored Rulers and lawful assistants, with the consent of the people..."* (Lutz, 4; emphasis added). At this early stage the people were already declaring that they would live under laws "consented by the people."

The purpose for discussing these early settlers and their documents is to show that these people came to the New World for varied reasons, some to make money and others for religious freedom. However, they all came with an understanding that forming a government that best suited the needs of their particular people, in their particular colony, was imperative. This idea of self-government was inherited from their Saxon forefathers who had established "witenagemots" or Parliaments in early Germania. These Saxons had developed a system that, as author Trevor Colbourn wrote, "Epitomized freedom, a freedom consisting of "being subject to no Law but such to which the Person who is bound consents" (Colburn, 38). As more and more disparate settlers came to the shores of America, different communities were created and different forms of government were chosen to fit their individual needs. These expanding communities eventually became thirteen separate and distinct colonies and eventually, States. The inhabitants of these colonies had differing ideas on how they wanted to manage their lives and developed governing bodies to reflect those ideas. New York, which was conquered from the Dutch in 1664, was no different. James, Duke of York and Albany was given proprietorship over most of the former Dutch colony. He immediately began to appoint governors and establish what would be called "The Dukes Laws" which centralized the government. However, because of the diverse makeup of the former Dutch colony, and since the Dutch were the majority of the settlers, it would be imprudent to form legislative assemblies as were appearing in the other British Colonies. These "Duke Laws" were "...broad regulations, leaving considerable room for discretion by local governments, church, and family. While clearly beginning the process of anglicizing both law and government in colonial New York, the laws more often than not deferred to community folkways and town and county governments" (Klein, 116).

In the process of forming new governments, these new inhabitants came to rely on some of the great political philosophers of the day, men like John Locke and Algernon

Sidney, John Trenchard and Thomas Gordon and later James Burgh, to help put their ideas into practice. These men, particularly John Locke, had a great impact on the emerging leaders of the colonies. Thomas Jefferson, while writing from Paris on February 15, 1789, considered John Locke as one of the "three greatest men that have ever lived" (Jefferson, 1002). Samuel Adams, eulogized by Boston's *Independent Chronicle* newspaper as the "Father of The Revolution" (Alexander, 221), was profoundly affected by John Locke. When attending school as a young man he kept a notebook with quotes from Locke including: "It is the right of the people to withdraw their support from that government which fails to fulfill its trust. If this does not persuade government to live up to its obligations, it is the right of the people to overthrow it" (Lewis, 7). To fully understand our form of government, we must understand those who created it and their influences.

The Philosophers

The importance of John Locke on those who created our system of government cannot be overstated. Almost every Founding Father quoted John Locke at some point in his career. Today, you would be hard pressed to find any book concerning the men who had a part in the creation and development of the Declaration of Independence, the Articles of Confederation or our current Constitution, which did not contain a reference to John Locke. Because of this influence it is imperative that we know who John Locke was and why he had such an impact on our consensual form of government.

John Locke was an English philosopher and physician who died in 1704 and wrote several pieces that were extremely influential on the founding generation, the most important being, "Two Treatises of Government." The writings by Locke would be quoted over and over again throughout the founding era and establish the foundation on which political societies were created. Locke believed that all men were born into a "State of Nature", a term widely used by the Founding generation. He wrote: "To understand Political power right, and derive it from its original, we must consider what state all men are naturally in, and that is, a state of perfect freedom to order their actions, and dispose of their possessions, and persons as they think fit, within the bounds of the Law of Nature, without asking leave, *or depending upon the will of any other man*" (Locke, 269 emphasis added). He believed that all men were born free to live their lives without interference from anyone and that they lived in "A state of equality, wherein all the power and jurisdiction is reciprocal, no one having more than another" (ibid, 269). Therefore, according to Locke, the definition of "State of Nature" was "Men living together according to reason, without a common Superior on Earth, with authority to judge between them" (ibid, 280). While in this state, the use of force, even deadly force, against another person is justified to defend ones property, within "reason." Locke writes: " Want of a common judge with authority, puts all men in a *State of Nature*: Force without right, upon a man's person, makes a *State of War*, both where there is, and is not, a common Judge" (ibid, 281). Locke understood that the State of Nature and eventually a State of War could be problematic. One man may not "reason" the same way as another and this could lead to violence and injury to innocent parties. Locke goes on to write: "Man being born as has been proved, with a title to perfect Freedom, and an uncontrolled enjoyment of all the rights and privileges of the Law of Nature, equally with any other man, or number of men in the world, hath by nature a power, not only to preserve his property, that is, his Life, Liberty and Estate, against the injuries and attempts of other men; but to judge of, and punish the breaches of that law in others, as he is persuaded the offense deserves, even with death itself, in crimes where the heinousness of the fact, in his opinion, requires it" (ibid, 323-324). He continues, "To avoid this State of War (wherein there is no appeal but to Heaven, and wherein every the least difference is apt to end, where there is no authority to decide between the contenders) is one great reason of men's putting themselves into Society, and quitting the State of Nature" (ibid, 282). So, according to Locke, man would leave their *State of Nature* and enter into *Political or Civil Society*. What was Locke's definition of this Political or Civil society? "Those who are united into one body, and have a common established Law and Judicature to appeal to, with authority to decide controversies between them and punish offenders, are in Civil Society one with another" and "Wherever therefore any number of men are so united into one society, as to quit every one his Executive Power of the Law of Nature, and to resign it to the public, there and there only is a Political, or Civil Society" (ibid, 324-325). John Locke believed man entered into a political society because it was a better way to protect and preserve his property than remaining in a *State of Nature*. The man who was leaving this State of Nature understood that he was giving up some of his inherent power to solely judge and execute laws that he believed to be within reason. He was subjecting himself to the Political Power of another; however, he did so with his own consent. This is the foundation of Locke's philosophy on Civil or Political society. He wrote, "The only way whereby any one divests himself of his Natural Liberty, and *puts on the bonds of Civil Society* is by agreeing with other men to join and unite into a community, for their comfortable, safe, and peaceable living one amongst another, in a secure Enjoyment of their properties, and a greater security against any that are not in it." This philosophy would become a main focal point of the colonies that wished to retain their liberty against the perceived threat of English tyranny. Nobody, King or other legislative body, had any authority to act contrary to the peoples wishes. The Colonies were created and eventually united, with the peoples consent and who gave up none of their inherent rights.

While Locke was arguably the most important philosopher of the time, many others also had immense influence on those creating new societies in America. One of those was Algernon Sidney, a British Politician and Republican theorist who was executed for his opposition to King Charles II in 1683. Sidney wrote "*Discourses Concerning Government*" which was a book of great importance to men like Thomas Jefferson, who even recommended Sidney as one of a few writers who could present an understanding of the "Organization of Society into a Civil Government" (Jefferson, 1182). Sidney wrote: "Man cannot continue in the…liberty that God hath given him. The liberty of one is thwarted by that of another; and whilst they are equal, none will yield to any, otherwise than by a general consent. This is the ground of all just government" (Sidney, 30-31). Once again, the belief in government only under the consent of the governed is considered a "Just government."

James Burgh, a British Whig politician and philosopher, was another who had an important influence. His book *Political Disquisitions* was widely read and included a chapter entitled "The People, the Fountain of Authority, the Object of Government, and the last Resource" begins, "All lawful authority, legislative, and executive, originates from the people. Power in the people is like light in the sun, native, original, inherent and unlimited by anything human. In governors, it may be compared to the reflected light of the moon, for it is only borrowed, delegated, and limited by the intention of the people, whose it is, and to whom governors are to consider themselves responsible, while the people are answerable only to God...As the people are the fountain of power, and object of government, so are they the last resource, when governors betray their trust" (Burgh, 3-4).

Cato's Letters, a series of essays written by John Trenchard and Thomas Gordon were indispensable to many of the founding era. They spoke out against government tyranny and of the blessings of individual freedom. In one essay, Gordon wrote: "Our lives and properties are secured by the best bulwark in the world, *that of laws made by ourselves, and executed by our magistrates, who are likewise made by us;* and when they are dishonestly executed, or willfully neglected, our constitution affords a remedy...And as no nation ever lost its liberty but by the force of foreign invaders, or the domestic treachery of its own magistrates" (Trenchard, 326 emphasis added).

There are many examples of this type of reasoning found throughout the writings of the founding generation. I include these examples as evidence that the founders of our Republic, agreeing with the likes of Locke, Sidney, Trenchard, Gordon and Burgh, held crucial the idea that any form of government could only be made with the consent of the people. The "people" consisted of those who had entered into distinct and separate societies that eventually became separate and distinct colonies and eventually States. No one would dare argue that these distinct peoples did not have the inherent right to govern themselves in the manner of their own choosing. They were uniquely different, and their people, leaving the "State of Nature" would decide for themselves how they would delegate authority.

The First Attempts at Confederation

The individual colonies had an amicable, yet sometimes contentious, relationship with each other. As early as 1643, Massachusetts, Connecticut, New Haven and Plymouth Colonies had formed the New England Confederation in order to settle border disputes along with trade and religious quarrels. However, the confederation was also formed for mutual defense against French, Indian and Dutch aggression. This type of relationship was typical throughout America, and mutual aid was discussed by the individual colonies on numerous occasions. Yet, it wasn't until 1754 that the thought of uniting all the colonies in a mutual defense agreement was considered. The Albany Congress or Albany Conference was the idea of Massachusetts Governor William Shirley and Benjamin Franklin. Once again fear played an important part for the notion of a confederation. The French were beginning to move into the Western territories, particularly the Ohio Valley, and had begun to seek help from the Iroquoian alliance. This threatened the lucrative fur trade and hindered further western settlement. Many of the colonies, particularly Virginia and New York, called for assistance from their sister colonies to put a halt to this French intrusion. However, getting that assistance was not going to be an easy task. While the colonies had cordial relationships with each other, they each had their own interest and involving themselves in a war with the French would be costly. In May of 1754, a friend of Franklin's, Doctor William Clarke of Boston, wrote to him worried over the French intrusion. In his letter the Doctor lamented that the Colonies needed to unite in order to save the continent for Great Britain but thought it unlikely to happen. Clarke wrote: "I cannot help thinking that unless there be a united and vigorous opposition of the English colonies…the French are laying a solid foundation for being…sole masters of this continent…but this union is hardly to be expected to be brought about by a confederacy or voluntary agreement, among ourselves. The jealousies the colonies have of each other…will effectually hinder anything of this kind from taking place…we should never agree about the form of the union or who should have the execution of the articles of it…" (Newbold, 32). Protection against the French and Indians was one thing, uniting with the other colonies and forming a Union was something else. Ironically, the British government liked the idea of a union. Thomas Robinson, Secretary of State for the Southern Department, endorsed the Albany Congress plan by writing to Governor Shirley, "… immediate directions will be given for promoting the plan of a general concert between his Majesty's colonies" (Newbold, 35). The British government, thousands of miles away, was beginning to worry about the French intrusion and wanted the colonies to act together in order to prevent them from becoming too powerful a threat. The Albany Congress was to be the first attempt to unite the colonies into a confederation. The plan was adopted by the delegates, However, it went nowhere in the colonial legislatures. Benjamin Franklin and William Shirley both wanted Parliament to push the Colonies into union, but nothing more was heard of the Albany Plan in England after it was discovered that the colonial assemblies almost unanimously rejected the plan. As Robert Newbold wrote: "The virtually unanimous rejection of the scheme by the provincial legislatures was probably reason enough to persuade the British government to drop any contemplated consideration of a project that had already aroused violent criticism in the colonies" (Newbold, 173). The idea of a confederation between all of the colonies had made its appearance. Many realized that some sort of defensive union would be necessary to prevent the French from becoming to powerful. However, the individual colonies were not ready to form a confederation with their sisters just yet. However, it would not be very long before a new scheme of confederation would take place. Once again, Benjamin Franklin would play an important role; however, this time it would not have the blessings of the British Crown

A Crisis Brews

After the defeat of the French during the so-called "French and Indian" War, the urgent need to confederate the colonies vanished. There always loomed the Indian threat of violence, but most colonies felt that this was something they could handle on their own. It would be another kind of threat that would spur the colonist to seek confederation, one that had its origins in the recent conflict. Great Britain was in fiscal trouble after the war. It was nearly bankrupt and felt that the colonist should pay their fair share of the burden. By attempting to raise revenue from the colonies against their will, a fire was being stoked that would eventually ignite and consume both nations and most of Europe. The crisis that brewed throughout the American colonies during the middle and latter parts of the 1760's, the Stamp Act and Townsend Acts, set the stage for the showdown with The King and Parliament that would eventually lead to the thirteen colonies declaring Independence and forming a more "permanent" union.

Today, it is hard for most people to understand that long

before our current Constitution was in effect, the States had their own Constitutions that governed their citizens' lives without any interference from a "National" government. Harking back to the formation of their individual communities that eventually evolved into Colonies and then States, these documents were tailored to their individual concerns and needs. So, before outright Independence was called for, the Colonies began to set the wheels in motion by creating these Constitutions and in effect declaring their independence. As Dr. James McClellan suggested, this was a monumental and historical occasion, He wrote: "...this was the first time in the world's history that a large group of communities—now thirteen independent and sovereign States —had begun the formation of their own governments under written Constitutions (McClellan 2000). In January and February of 1776, New Hampshire and South Carolina created the first two State Constitutions, which were considered only temporary. A peace with Great Britain was still thought possible, and each only lasted a few years. Rhode Island and Connecticut kept their charter governments and Massachusetts kept its charter government temporarily. New Jersey also created their Constitution prior to the Declaration of Independence and on May 15, 1776, nearly two months before the united States declared their independence from Great Britain, the Colony of Virginia adopted several independent resolutions that effectively made them an independent and sovereign State. While other colonies were creating documents to govern themselves during the present crisis, Virginia ratified what would be, as Dr. Kevin Gutzman wrote, "the first permanent constitution framed by the people's representatives in world history (Gutzman, 8). Virginia's model, like several others, contained a Bill of Rights which secured such things as, freedom of religion, the press and the right to keep and bear arms. All of the States clearly recognized that they were no longer part of the British Empire and by creating Constitutions and declaring themselves independent they acted as sovereign entities, never considering themselves as one giant State.

These newly independent States realized that by seceding from Great Britain they were going to incur the wrath of the Crown who saw these colonies, not as sovereign and independent, but as rebels. The States knew that they were on their own and would need to form some kind of defensive treaty with each other in order to survive the coming onslaught of British military might. To make their split with England official, precedent dictated that they declare to the world the reasons which impel them to the separation.

Independent and Sovereign

When the Declaration of Independence was written and then declared to the world the signatories made it perfectly clear for whom they were speaking and what was intended: "We, therefore, the representatives of the United States of America, in General Congress assembled, appealing to the Supreme Judge of the world ... *do, in the name and by the authority of the good people of these colonies* solemnly publish and declare, That these United Colonies are, and of right ought to be, *FREE AND INDEPENDENT STATES*; that they are absolved from all allegiance to the British crown and that all political connection between them and the state of Great Britain is, and ought to be, totally dissolved; and that, *as free and independent states*, they have full power to levy war, conclude peace, contract alliances, establish commerce, and do all other acts and things *which independent states may of right do*. And for the support of this declaration, with a firm reliance on the protection of Divine Providence, we mutually pledge to each other our lives, our fortunes, and our sacred honor."

It is clear that the men who declared their independence from Great Britain considered themselves as citizens of "free and Independent States" and could act as such on par with the other nations of the earth. They could "levy war" and "conclude peace" like all other sovereign nations. Conservatives, like Joseph Galloway of Pennsylvania, who had fought against declaring independence, now knew that a radical departure had taken place. The Conservatives believed that all political authority came from a higher power, namely the King and Parliament, not the people. As Merrill Jensen writes: "When independence became a fact, they (the Conservatives) were forced to accept the theoretical foundation of the Revolution, the doctrine of the sovereignty of the people, which at the time was understood to be *the people organized as states*, not the people organized in a nation known as the "United States" (Jensen, The Articles of Confederation, 165).

Now that they were fully independent, the States (or individual Nations)[2] knew that individually they would be no match for the mighty military machine of Great Britain. In order to sustain their independence they would need to form a defensive Confederation. As with prior attempts at confederation, delegates from the several States would need to meet to hash out some type of formal rules for governance.

---

[2] A **sovereign state** is a state with a defined territory on which it exercises internal and external sovereignty, a permanent population, a government, independence from other states and powers, and the capacity to enter into relations with other sovereign states. It is also normally understood to be a state which is not dependent on, or subject to any other power or state. Shaw, Malcolm Nathan (2003). *International law.* Cambridge University Press

The Articles of Confederation would be the document that officially brought into being the entity called the United States of America; however it would not be an easy task.

A committee was formed, led by John Dickinson of Pennsylvania, which was entrusted to come up with a plan of confederation. After many delays, Dickinson had come up with a plan that considerably strengthened the Continental Congress. Almost immediately this plan was rejected, most notably by Thomas Burke of North Carolina, and Dickinson's Union was reduced to a "league of friendship." According to Forrest McDonald, "Dickinson's article granting broad powers to Congress was replaced by Burke's article reserving sovereignty and independence to the several states" (Mc Donald, States Rights And The Union 1776-1876, 38-39). After much wrangling, particularly about ownership of the Western lands, a plan was unanimously (which was necessary under the Articles) adopted on March 1, 1781.

The first article of the Articles of Confederation states: "The Stile of this confederacy shall be "The United States of America." Note that the delegates thought of the union of states as a "Confederation." The definition of confederation according to Webster's New World Dictionary is as follows: 1). a uniting or being united in a league or alliance. 2).a league or alliance; specif., independent nations or states joined in a league or confederacy whose central authority is usually confined to common defense or foreign relations.[3] Once again, the delegates understood that they were committing themselves to a union with other sovereign entities that would have the benefit of common defense and

---

[3] Webster's New World Dictionary of The American Language, Second College Edition Simon & Schuster

trade. As Thomas Jefferson made clear, Virginia was "one of thirteen nations, who have agreed to act together" (Gutzman, 63). To make certain that each state understood the relationship, they included the second article, which read: ***"Each State retains its sovereignty, freedom, and independence, and every power, jurisdiction and right, which is not by this confederation expressly delegated to the United States, in Congress assembled."***

There can be no doubt; the States were not giving up any of their sovereign rights, only those that were delegated, nor their independence when contemplating joining the confederation. As stated earlier, this new constitution could only take effect after all thirteen States agreed to ratify it. Of course there were many complications and it would take almost four years to ratify, verifying that the States were extremely jealous of their newly declared independence. At the time they were still fighting a war against what they considered a tyrannical central government and they wanted to make certain that they were not just exchanging tyrants.

As has been shown so far, the states evolved from communities that were unique and independent. For nearly 175 years they cherished this uniqueness and avoided becoming entangled with their sister's except when necessary for defense against hostile Indians, the French, the Dutch and eventually their own kinsman from Great Britain. Several attempts at confederation amounted to very little until their very survival required it. They each had declared their sovereign independence, as shown in the Declaration of Independence, fought a long and bloody war, established a common government under the Articles of Confederation that saw them through that war, and now had won the right to make peace with the King on their terms.

The Definitive Treaty of Peace 1783, better known as the Treaty of Paris, was the agreement between Great Britain and the United States of America that ended our war for independence. His Majesty, King George III, ended the war by signing a peace treaty that recognized the individual, sovereign states of America. Article I of the treaty states: "His Britannic Majesty acknowledges the said United States, viz., New Hampshire, Massachusetts Bay, Rhode Island and Providence Plantations, Connecticut, New York, New Jersey, Pennsylvania, Maryland, Virginia, North Carolina, South Carolina and Georgia, to be free sovereign and independent states, that he treats with them as such, and for himself, his heirs, and successors, relinquishes all claims to the government, propriety, and territorial rights of the same and every part thereof" (Library 2008).

After eight bitter and bloody years of fighting, the several States of America had persevered and had their independence secured. It was not a consolidated nation, made up of one people, which was recognized by King George, it was thirteen independent and sovereign States.

After the war, with no more foreign enemy to fight, the states resumed the bickering between each other over things such as commerce, taxes, Western lands and tariffs. Even the Continental Congress was losing its luster, and hardly met any longer. Between October 1, 1785 and April 30, 1786, nine States-the minimum required to do any serious business-were represented on only three days (Mc Donald, 237). In order for the Union to survive, some changes were going to be needed, and more importantly, Congress needed money in order to pay its bills.

For many, the Articles of Confederation provided a sufficient government, one that had got them through a bloody conflict against the most powerful nation on Earth and which united a diverse population scattered over thousands of miles. However, most people recognized that a stronger central government was needed if their confederation was to continue. In 1783, Congress had requested an impost amendment that would have allowed it to collect import revenue directly from the States. The amendment lingered for many years, frustrated by several of the States, particularly New York, which was very protective of her commercial interest. In 1786, Charles Pinckney of South Carolina, a member of Congress tried to force a floor vote with the idea of calling for a Constitutional Convention. He sought changes to the Articles that would strengthen Congress, but was soundly defeated. As Professor James McClellan wrote, "The American nation was still thought of as a group of nation-states, and the members of Congress were reluctant to surrender their power voluntarily" (McClellan, 163).

The States were once again looking out for their own interest and Congress seemed powerless to provide leadership to the union. However, it would be the States in their sovereign capacity that would get things going. Maryland and Virginia, taking the initiative, settled a long-standing commercial dispute without the help of Congress. Buoyed by the successful completion of the agreement, Maryland's leaders initiated a call for a convention with Border States Delaware and Pennsylvania, hoping to accomplish another inter-state commercial agreement. Virginia agreed and in March of 1786, Patrick Henry, the fiery Governor of Virginia, assented to the wishes of his Assembly and sent out a circular letter to his fellow governors requesting that all the States should send delegates to this proposed "commercial convention" in

Annapolis, Maryland on the first Monday in September (Mc Donald, 239).The hope was that some agreement could be made to regulate the commercial interest of the confederation by strengthening the hand of Congress. This would also add much needed revenue to the government's coffers. Alas, it was not meant to be. Only five States sent delegates and the Annapolis Convention was a failure. However, from the ashes a new idea arose. James Madison and Alexander Hamilton attempted to convince the attending delegates to seek another attempt at a convention the following May. They agreed unanimously to try. Congress, probably believing it was a fruitless endeavor, refused to give its approval. Once again, Virginia's legislature took the lead and issued a resolution calling on all the States to send delegates to, what would become, the Philadelphia Convention. With several States committing themselves to this new attempt at a convention, Congress finally relented. James McClellan writes: "Perceiving the inevitable, a reluctant Congress adopted without reference to the Annapolis recommendation, its own resolution providing for a convention to meet at the same time and place" (McClellan, 163).

The States Call for a Convention

The States, in their sovereign capacity, had agreed to send delegates to a convention seeking to amend the Articles of Confederation. It seemed too many that this may be the last chance to get a fruitful agreement amongst the States and to strengthen and preserve the Union. Not all were happy about calling for a new Convention, particularly Patrick Henry. He believed that the Articles of Confederation were sufficient, albeit that some minor changes may be necessary. He refused to attend the Convention reportedly saying: "I smelt a rat" (Mc Donald, E Pluribus Unum: The Formation of The

American Republic 1776-1790, 260).

"On Monday the 14th of May, A.D. 1787, and in the eleventh year of the independence of the United States of America… *in virtue of appointments from their respective states*, sundry Deputies to the Federal-Convention appeared-but, *a majority of the States not being represented*, the members present adjourned…until Friday the 25th of the said month…" (Farrand, The Records of the Federal Convention of 1787 v.I, 1 Emphasis added). So began the attempt at strengthening the Union. Once again, it is noteworthy that it was the States, not the whole people, who made the appointment of Delegates. Because a majority of the "States" was not present, the convention could not continue. It is crucial to the understanding of our system of government that one recognize that the States in their sovereign capacity authorized this convention. Instead, many would claim, and still do, that it was the mass of people of the combined States, not of the individual States, who authorized it. Nothing could be further from the truth; the people of Rhode Island were not even represented!

When the Convention opened on May 25th the note-takers made it a point to establish right away who was calling for a convention. Robert Yates of New York began his notes: "Attended the convention *of the states*, at the state house in Philadelphia, when the following states were represented…" (ibid, 5 Emphasis added). These delegates were authorized by their States to attend a convention in order to amend the Articles of Confederation. That they overstepped their authority is not the topic of this paper. However, the one thing that becomes evident throughout the debates is the fact that these men will have to put together a form of government that will be supported by the people who sent them. Without this support, no system could prevail and all would be for naught. They were currently in a confederation, and a confederation they would remain.

Several of the Delegates would submit plans for a new system of government. Edmund Randolph of Virginia would be one of the first. "Mr. Randolph... laid before the House... sundry propositions, in writing concerning the american confederation..." (ibid,16). Charles Pinckney of South Carolina would be another to submit plans for a federal government "to be agreed upon between the free and independent States of America" (ibid, 16).

While several more plans would be debated, it was Randolph's "Virginia" plan that would get the most attention and which would be the basis, after much debate and revision, for what would ultimately become our Federal Constitution. So what were Randolph's objectives? "He observed that in *revising the federal system* (Articles of Confederation) we ought to inquire 1.Into the properties, which a government ought to possess, 2.The defects of the *Confederation,* 3.The danger of our situation and 4.The remedy." When answering his own question as to what properties the new government should posses, Randolph said, "to be paramount to the state constitutions" (ibid. 18 Emphasis added). Robert Yates of New York, a future New York Supreme Court Justice, took his own notes during the convention and knew exactly what Randolph was recommending. He wrote of Randolph and his resolves, "He candidly confessed that they were not intended for a federal government-he meant a strong *consolidated* union, in which the idea of states should be nearly annihilated" (ibid, 24). Yates knew that there were many in attendance who, like Randolph, wished for an all powerful *National* government instead of a Federal government, a

National government that would be supreme in all cases and which would make the States subservient to its will. Randolph was arguing that the current Confederation was too weak and was "incompetent to any one object for which it was instituted." He understood that it was the States who held most of the power, and this is what he believed was hampering the effectiveness of the Articles of Confederation. James McHenry, a delegate from Maryland, wrote in his notes Randolph's list of objections to the current Articles, one being that "It is not superior to State constitutions" and that "No judge will say that the confederation is paramount to a State constitution" (ibid, 26).

This would be the crucial topic of the Convention. Would the delegates create an all-powerful National government, in which the States were basically abolished, or would they adhere to the idea of a Federal government, in which the States were the integral pieces of the whole? The debate raged on.

First it had to be understood what the delegates believed was meant by a "Federal" or "National, Supreme" government. Gouverneur Morris, from Pennsylvania, gave his explanation, "the former being a mere compact resting on the good faith of the parties; the latter having a compleat and compulsive operation. He contended that in all communities there must be one supreme power, and one only" (ibid, 34). James Madison observed "that whatever reason might have existed for the equality of suffrage when the Union was a *federal one among sovereign States*, it must cease when a national government should be put into place" (ibid, 37 Emphasis added).

A resolve was placed before the Convention: "That a union of the states merely federal, will not accomplish the objects proposed by the articles of the confederation, namely, common defense, security of liberty, and general welfare." During the consideration of this first resolve Mr. Charles Cotesworth Pinckney[4] observed "that if the convention agreed to it, it appeared to him that their business was at an end; for as the powers of the house in general were to revise the present confederation, and to alter or amend it as the case might require; to determine its insufficiency or incapability of amendment or improvement, must end in the dissolution of powers" (ibid, 39). Pinckney knew that if the idea was to change the government from a Federal to a National one, they might as well have ended the Convention right then and there. He had no authority to agree to such a change. The resolve was dropped, for the moment. Noteworthy, however, was the underlying object of the resolve, namely the "common defense, security of liberty, and general welfare" of the union. These are very limited goals and are stated throughout the Convention as to the reason for a confederation in the first place. The third resolve stated: "That a national government ought to be established, consisting of a supreme judicial, legislative and executive" which, like the first resolve, ran into difficulties. "The term "supreme" required an explanation- It was asked whether it was intended to annihilate state governments? It was answered, only so far as the powers intended to be granted to the new government should clash with the States, when the latter was to yield" (ibid, 39).

---

[4] Charles Pickney and Brig. General Charles Cotesworth Pinkney were cousins from South Carolina, Cotesworth being the elder of the two. A note in Farrand, Volume I, page 39, notes: Madison and McHenry ascribe expressions of certain notes to Gen. C.C. Pinckney. Yates does not always distinguish between the two.

The "Nationalists", those seeking a National government, were put in the spotlight. Were they trying to abolish the state governments and make the new government "Supreme" in all matters? No, they claimed. But they were not being very truthful. It was only May and there was still nearly four more months of debates left for them to figure out a way to sneak in a plan for a supreme, national government. They did not give up hope.

On June 19th, Alexander Hamilton gave a speech that laid out his scheme for an all-powerful National government that would, for all intents and purposes, dissolve the State governments. He admitted that "different societies have different views and interests to pursue, and always prefer local to general concerns" (ibid, 295). He felt that it was the Federal government that was in danger of being swallowed up by the States whose local concerns would always outweigh National concerns. His idea would be for a Chief Executive and Senate that would be elected for life. His Chief Executive would have "the power of negativing all laws-to make war or peace, with the advice of the Senate-to make treaties with their advice, but to have sole direction of all military operations…"(ibid, 300-301). His model legislature would appoint courts in each state "so as to make the state governments unnecessary to it" and "All state laws to be absolutely void which contravene the general laws" (ibid, 301).

However, he knew that this was only a dream. "I confess that this plan and that of Virginia are very remote from the idea of the people" (ibid, 301). Samuel Johnson of Connecticut was observed saying that "The Gentleman from NYk is praised by every gentleman, but supported by no gentleman" (ibid, 366). Even a Nationalist like James Wilson knew that a plan such

34

as Hamilton's would never be accepted. Wilson observed "that by a Natl. Govt. we did not mean one that would swallow up the State Govts. As seemed to be wished by some gentleman. He was tenacious of the idea of preserving the latter. He thought, contrary to the opinion of (Col. Hamilton) that they might (not) only subsist but subsist on friendly terms with the former. They were absolutely necessary for certain purposes which the former could not reach" (ibid, 323). It was on these "certain purposes" that the Nationalists and Federalists disagreed. Luther Martin of Maryland, a fierce advocate of the sovereignty of the States, made it clear how he felt: "When the States threw off their allegiance on Great Britain, they became independent of her and each other. They united and confederated for mutual defense, and this was done on principles of perfect reciprocity. They will now again meet on the same ground. But when dissolution takes place, our rights and sovereignties are resumed. Our accession to the union has been by the states. If any other principle is adopted by this convention, he will give it every opposition" (ibid, 329).

Martin's "Original" or "Natural" right thinking is taken straight from John Locke. James Wilson and Alexander Hamilton disagreed. So the debate raged. On July 5th, Robert Yates and John Lansing of New York abruptly left the Convention. The two New Yorkers were ardent Anti-Nationalist and felt that the Convention was overstepping its bounds. In a letter to Governor Clinton they explained their reasons for leaving the Convention. First, they had been appointed to "revise the Articles of Confederation, not to draw up a new constitution as the Convention decided to do. Secondly, they disapproved of the consolidation of the United States into one national state, for it would subvert the

Constitution of New York and impair its sovereignty" (Spaulding, 189).

Although James Wilson was a Nationalist, he was beginning to see the writing on the wall. It appeared that the true Federalists would not give up, so the next best thing would be to try and water down the power of the State governments. Wilson argued, like Hamilton, that it was the National government that should be fearful of the States. However, it was time to start looking for some type of compromise, "But let us try to designate the powers of each, and then no danger can be apprehended nor can the general government be possessed of any ambitious views to encroach on the state rights" (Farrand, The Records of the Federal Convention of 1787 v.I, 363).James Madison, still trying to have a Supreme National government, would not yield, "I apprehend the greatest danger is from the encroachment of the States on the National government...The right of negativing in *certain* instances the state laws, affords one security to the national government" (ibid, 363 Emphasis added). While Madison was still championing a Supreme government, his tone altered slightly. Instead of having the national government negate *all* state laws, he now advocated the negating of only *certain* laws. The Nationalists were clearly on the defensive now. Instead of trying to abolish the State governments, they would try and show that their plans were to keep the States and only give that power which was absolutely necessary for the protection of the National government. Again, Samuel Johnson was quoted as saying, "If the advocates for the Genl. Govt. agreeably to the Virgin. Plan can show that the State Govts. will be secure from the Genl. Govt. we may all agree-"(ibid, 366).

Oliver Ellsworth, known as Judge Ellsworth in the debates,

was another who knew that his State of Connecticut would never allow the abolishment of the State governments. In fact he understood that it was the States who were forming this government in the first place. Would it be reasonable that any state would vote to abolish itself? He reminded the other delegates "that without their [the States] approbation your government is nothing more than a rope of sand" (ibid, 379). As the summer wore on, it became obvious that the States would remain an integral part of any new government, whether they called it Federal of National, it did not really make much of a difference. The Federal government was only to possess those powers which were necessary for national objects. On July 12, Gouverneur Morris spoke after a debate raged over the Southern States' proposal to include their Negro population for representation purposes. The speech is important because it highlights the purpose of the Convention. Many came with the express direction of the States who sent them to amend the Articles of Confederation; the two New Yorkers had left over this issue. However, there was little doubt amongst most that the Central government needed more power to keep the Union intact. On the other hand, there were those, like Hamilton, and in the beginning Madison, who sought a total weakening and even abolishment of the States. What did Morris say? According to James Madison's notes it was this, "It has been said that it is high time to speak out...He came here to form a compact for the good of America. He was ready to do so with all the States: He hoped and believed that all would enter into such a compact. If they would not he was ready to join with any States that would. *But as the Compact was to be voluntary*, it is in vain for the Eastern States to insist on what the Southern States will never agree to" (ibid, 593 Emphasis added). The new government was to be a "Voluntary Compact" between

States. The States would join the Union or not, they would not be forced. Still arguing over the role of slavery and the Negro population, Rufus King of Massachusetts feared the day when the Southern States would be more numerous than those in the North. A few Southern Delegates had threatened to leave the Union over the Slavery issue. King was noted as saying, "If they threaten to separate now in case injury shall be done them, will their threats be less urgent or effectual, when force shall back their demands. Even in the intervening period there will be no point of time at which they will not be able to say, *do us justice or we will separate*" (ibid, 596 Emphasis added). Nearly eighty years later a President elected by a minority of the people, of one section of the country, would claim that the Union was indissolvable and perpetual. It seems that he was wrong. It was understood by all, nobody objected to either King's or Morris' statements, that this Union was voluntary.

On September 17th the Convention came to a close. The new Constitution was read aloud and the remaining Delegates, with the exception of Edmund Randolph, George Mason and Elbridge Gerry, signed the document. It was not perfect. The Nationalist had fought hard for an all-powerful National government and the Anti-Nationalist fought just as hard to retain the Sovereignty of the States. Roger Sherman of Connecticut had explained it in plain terms: "Few objects, then will be before the Genl. Government-foreign War, Treaties of commerce &c-in short let the Genl. Government be a sort of collateral Government which shall secure the States in particular difficulties such as foreign war, or war between two or more States" (ibid, 142-143). It was to be a limited government, with only certain delegated powers that pertained to "National" objectives only. The convention was over, but the battle had just begun. It was now up to the States, in their sovereign capacity, to decide if this was truly a government that would secure their liberty and be worth joining or if it was a Tyrant in disguise.

The States Decide

The Constitution that was agreed upon by the Convention Delegates formed a Federal style government. According to James McClellan, " Federalism may be defined as a system of government in which there are two levels of authority, national and state, operating side by side, with each level generally supreme within its sphere of power"(McClellan, 297). This is basically the same definition that Thomas Jefferson gave, describing the Constitution as a "compact of the several States in which they agreed to unite in a single government as to their relations with each other and with foreign nations, and as to other articles particularly specified…but retained at the same time, each to itself, the other rights of independent government comprehending mainly their domestic interest" (Mayer, 185).

The States, in their sovereign capacity, were the entities that were going to decide if this Constitution and its federal style government were to go into effect. There is absolutely no reason to believe, as many later claimed and still do, that the American people as a whole were going to decide the outcome. After listing the names of twelve of the thirteen States (Rhode Island did not send Delegates), it was resolved that "the preceding Constitution be laid before the United States in congress assembled…that it should be submitted to a Convention of Delegates, chosen in each State by the People thereof, under the Recommendation of its Legislature, for the Assent and Ratification…." Nine States would suffice to begin operation of the new government. The debates during the States ratifying conventions are extremely important for understanding our system of government, because it would rest on them to decide whether or not the Constitution and the Union would live or die.

Some States began forming ratifying Conventions almost immediately but others took their time. The first State to ratify was Delaware, then Pennsylvania and New Jersey. All ratified by the end of December, 1787. Early January, 1788 saw Connecticut and Georgia ratify. The next state, Massachusetts, was an important one. It had been mentioned that without Massachusetts, Virginia and New York, there could be no Union even if nine other States ratified. Elbridge Gerry was back from the convention voicing his concerns, his main one being a lack of a Bill of Rights, and he had the ear of his mentor, the man Thomas Jefferson called "truly the Man of the Revolution", Samuel Adams (Stoll, 8). Adams had been instrumental in helping draft the Massachusetts Constitution and the new Federal Constitution was very similar. However, Adams was very jealous of the sovereignty of his State and recognized that without a Bill of Rights and the seeming consolidation of the States, that sovereignty would be destroyed. He voiced his concerns in a letter to his friend, Richard Henry Lee, on December 3, 1787: "If the several States of the Union are to become one entire Nation, under one Legislature, the Powers of which shall extend to every Subject of Legislation, and its Laws be supreme & control the whole, the Idea of Sovereignty in these States must be lost... But should we continue distinct sovereign States, confederated for the purpose of mutual safety and Happiness, each contributing to the Federal Head such a part of its sovereignty as would render the Government fully adequate to those purposes and no more, the People would govern themselves more easily, the Laws of each State being well adapted to its own genius & circumstances..." (Ibid, 230-231). With such a Patriot voicing his concerns over the new Government, the so-called "Federalists" (those in favor of ratifying the Constitution), needed to convince him and his followers, that the new government was not an all powerful consolidated government. John Hancock, the Governor of Massachusetts, was a trusted and long time friend of Samuel Adams. The two had had a falling out, but now were both committed to ensuring that if the new Constitution was to be ratified it must protect the liberties of the people and the sovereignty of the States. Hancock, who had been ill, made it to the Convention on January 31, where he proceeded to recommend nine amendments to the Constitution. Among them were the right to a jury trial in civil actions, restricting Congress's direct taxation powers, barring Congress from creating companies that have exclusive advantages, and stating "that it be explicitly declared, that all powers not expressly delegated to Congress, are reserved to the several states, to be by them exercised" (Kaminski, Ratification of the Constitution by the States: Massachusetts, 1381).

The Amendments were something that many "Anti-Federalists" (a misnomer that described those who were leery of the new Constitution) wanted inserted before ratification. It was only with this compromise that enough votes were garnered for ratification. Even with the backing of Samuel Adams and John Hancock, ratification only prevailed by nineteen votes. Without the Amendments it is quite possible that ten "Anti-Federalists" would have voted not to ratify and Massachusetts would have remained out of the Union. However, Massachusetts was the sixth State to ratify leaving only three more to secure a new Government. It would take until June 21, 1788 for the magic number of nine to be attained. Maryland, South Carolina and then New Hampshire ratified and a new government was born. However, mighty Virginia had not yet ratified, nor had New York. Without Virginia it has been claimed, the new Union had no hopes of surviving.

On June 2, 1788 the Virginia Ratification Convention opened. As Professor Gutzman wrote, "When it came to the place of their state in the North American world, Virginians displayed little false modesty. Many assumed their verdict on the proposed constitution would be decisive" (Gutzman, 84). Giants of the Founding Era attended the convention; Patrick Henry, James Madison, George Mason and Edmund Randolph. These men represented both sides of the debate. Henry and Mason were staunch Republicans or "Anti-Federalists." Madison and Randolph were Federalists; however, Randolph had refused to sign the new Constitution when the Convention had ended in September. Both Randolph and Mason had argued for a Bill of Rights to be included in the document during the Constitutional Convention and this would be a sticking point now. Patrick Henry, who some said was the greatest orator of the generation; spoke early on about his uneasiness of their endeavor to change their form of government. While he was an advocate of a stronger central government he felt that the new constitution afforded little protection for the rights and liberties of Virginians. Henry spoke, "The public mind, as well as my own, is extremely uneasy at the proposed change of Government. Give me leave to form one of the number of those who wish to be thoroughly acquainted with the reasons of this perilous and uneasy situation-and why we are brought hither to decide on this great national question" (Kaminski, Ratification of the Constitution by the States: Virginia, 929). Henry was fearful, as many "Anti-Federalist" were, that the new government was going to destroy the sovereignty of the states by forming a consolidated nation. His speech continued, "…I would make this inquiry of those worthy characters who composed…the late Federal Convention. I am sure they were fully impressed with the necessity of forming a great Consolidated Government, instead of a confederation. That this is a Consolidated government is demonstrably clear…I have the highest veneration for those Gentlemen-but, Sir, give me leave to demand what right had they to say, *We, the People*…who authorized them to speak the language of, We, the People, instead of We, the States?" (ibid, 930). Henry had thrown down the gauntlet. It was now up to the Federalists to convince the other delegates that they were *not* forming a "Consolidated" government. A compromise was needed if Virginia was going to ratify the Constitution and the Federalists thought they had a solution. The Virginia Ratification would include a statement that would guarantee all that the "Anti-Federalists" desired. George Nicholas a Federalist and a friend of James Madison, made it clear that Virginia would retain its sovereignty, was delegating only certain power, and could resume it whenever it deemed that the Constitution had been perverted. Mister Nicholas contended "that the language of the proposed ratification, would secure every thing which Gentlemen desired, as it declared that all powers vested in the Constitution were derived from the people, and might be resumed by them whensoever they should be perverted to their injury and oppression; and that every power not granted thereby, remained at their will, no danger whatever could arise. For says he, these expressions will become a *part of the contract*.

43

The Constitution cannot be binding on Virginia, but with these conditions" (ibid, 1506 Emphasis added). Edmund Randolph was instrumental in getting the statement included into the Ratification agreement. Professor Gutzman writes, "According to Randolph's private reckoning at the time the Federalists won five delegates votes by his gambit, which makes it a decisive factor in securing ratification in Virginia" (Gutzman, 87). On June 25th it may indeed have been decisive, because the final tally for ratification was eighty-nine to seventy-nine. Five votes the other way would have sunk the Constitution in Virginia.

It is clear so far that the Constitution and its new form of government was not a forgone conclusion. Some of the smaller States, jealous of their sovereignty, nevertheless felt secure enough to ratify. The "Large" States had much more to loose and wanted their rights and liberties secured before entering any new Union. The idea that the Constitution was flawed for lacking a Bill of Rights, was indeed, the main sticking point for States like Massachusetts and Virginia. New York had opened its Convention on June 17th and was still debating when word had arrived in Poughkeepsie, the town where the Ratification debate was taking place, that nine States had ratified (it was not known right away that Virginia had ratified) and the new government was in effect for those States. The Anti-Federalists had a clear majority in the New York Convention and it had seemed that there was little chance that the Constitution would be ratified. When word had come that New Hampshire ratified and had given the new government an opportunity to go into effect, the situation drastically changed. The question now was whether or not New York would remain *out* of the union.

Once again, the main sticking point was the lack of a Bill of

Rights and Amendments that were felt needed to secure the rights and liberties of New Yorkers. The Anti-Federalists had an overwhelming majority at the outset of the Convention, forty-six to nineteen, and it was thought that the Federalists had little chance of success. It was reported that on February 7th, a group of approximately six hundred Anti-Federalists publicly burned a copy of the Constitution in the Town of Montgomery, located in Ulster County (Kaminski, Ratification of the Constitution by the States, 802). Leading the charge against ratification was the Governor, George Clinton, who happened to be from Ulster County. His fellow Anti-Federalists included men like John Lansing Jr. and Robert Yates, both of whom attended the Federal Convention but left early, and Melancton Smith from Dutchess County. Clinton was a man who felt strongly about the sovereignty of his State and believed that New York with its wealth of land, rivers and great port would sacrifice much by joining this new Union. On the Federalist side, men like Alexander Hamilton, who also attended the Federal Convention, John Jay and the wealthy Robert R. Livingston, chancellor of the State, would try to persuade enough delegates that the fate of the State and quite possibly the Union, rested on their deliberations. Hamilton clearly held no esteem for the rights of the States as his speech in the Federal Convention had proved.

However, all involved began to realize that some sought of compromise was going to be needed. On July 17th, *The New York Daily Advertiser* noted that a few days earlier, Alexander Hamilton had introduced a plan for ratification that was nearly similar to the one Virginia had presented but containing more declarations (Kaminski, Ratification, 2174-2175). It was at this time that it became known that Virginia had ratified with its Statement of Ratification, much like

Massachusetts, and proposed amendments to be submitted to the first Congress. Now the pressure was on for both sides. Some Federalists of the lower portion of the State, which included New York City and its Port, threatened to secede from the rest of the State and join the Union if ratification failed. John Jay spoke, "An idea has taken air that the southern part of the State will at all events, adhere to the Union; and, if necessary to that end, seek a separation from the northern. This idea has influence on the fears of the northern" (Spaulding, 254-255). Secession was not an idle threat. It was something the people understood as their inherent right to govern themselves as they saw fit.

Back and forth the debates continued until a compromise was reached. New York would ratify the Constitution by the slimmest of margins, thirty to twenty-seven, showing how strong the objections to the new Constitution were, however, their ratification would contain a Declaration of Rights, a Form of Ratification and recommendations for Amendments to the Constitution much like Virginia and Massachusetts had done. The Statement made clear that it was the "People of the State of New York" who were agreeing to this Union, "duly elected" and having "maturely considered" the Constitution. It was understood that it was not a consolidated nation of people who were deciding this momentous event, but the people of the individual States, in their sovereign capacity. It was further stated, "That the Powers of Government may be reassumed by the People, whensoever it shall become necessary to their Happiness; that every Power, Jurisdiction and right, which is not by the said Constitution clearly delegated to the Congress of the United States, or the departments of the Government thereof, remains to the People of the several States, or to their respective State

Governments to whom they have granted the same." It could not be made much clearer than that, the people of the States could resume their sovereignty if they so chose. The Union would remain a Confederation of Sovereign entities, not a consolidated National government. As per the wishes of the Convention, a circular letter went out to the other states requesting that amendments be adopted at the earliest convenience. It stated, "Several Articles in it appear so exceptionable to a Majority of us, that nothing but the fullest confidence, of obtaining a Revision of them, by a General Convention, and an invincible reluctance to separating from our Sister States could have prevailed upon a sufficient Number to ratify it, without stipulating for previous Amendments" (Kaminski, Ratification of The Constitution by The States XXIII, 2335). The feeling was that without amendments, the Government was flawed, and this needed to be corrected as quickly as possible.

With the ratification of New York and Virginia, it was felt that the Union would survive. However, not all the States had agreed to join. North Carolina had a fierce debate during its two Conventions and did not ratify for more than a year after New York. A history of civil unrest by the "Regulators" who felt that the State government favored the Tidewater Gentry caused many to loathe a stronger central government. Samuel Spencer, a state superior court judge and Anti-Federalist, had many objections to the new Constitution. One of these objections was that "There is no declaration of rights, to secure to every member of the society those unalienable rights which ought not to be given up to any government" , however, his Federalist opponents insisted that the States retained all power not formally granted to the new government (Maier, 417). James Iredell, a leading Federalist, seemed despondent when writing to his wife during the debates, "We are…for the present out of the Union…and God knows when we shall get in to it again" (ibid, 423). North Carolina was not in the Union but had retained its sovereignty. The question now was, like New York before it, whether they would join the Union or not. It seemed that, as with several of her sister States, the Anti-Federalists wanted Amendments before ratifying. New York's circular letter had been well received by many of the States and North Carolina was no different. When it finally ratified it included Amendments for consideration, the first being: "THAT each state in the union shall, respectively, retain every power, jurisdiction and right, which is not by this constitution delegated to the Congress of the United States, or to the departments of the Federal Government" (Ratification of the Constitution by the State of North Carolina 2011). Once again, it was noted that only limited powers would be delegated to the new Government and everything else was retained by the States.

Rhode Island was the last of the thirteen to ratify, nearly two years after New York. When it finally agreed to join the Union it too made sure that there was no doubt as to what kind of relationship it was entering into. On June 16th, 1790, a ratification notice was sent to Congress containing the following: "We, the delegates of the People of Rhode Island…make known… I. That there are certain natural rights of which men, when they form a social compact, cannot deprive or divest their posterity, - among which are the enjoyment of Life and liberty… II. That the powers of government may be resumed by the people whensoever it shall become necessary to their happiness" (Elliot, 334). The relationship was a compact between Sovereign States that could be ended when they deemed it necessary.

Time after time we see the States declaring the fact that they were sovereign. This was a cornerstone of the Articles of Confederation, and although it was not an expressed part of the Constitution drafted at the Federal Convention, the States made sure that it would be. The debates of the several State conventions made it clear that while most believed a stronger central government was needed, the Sovereignty of the States would not be abolished. Only those powers needed for the functioning of the National government would be relinquished by the States. On December 15th, 1791, the States ratified what would become the Bill of Rights. These first ten amendments were the culmination of what the Anti-Federalists fought so hard to achieve. To make it perfectly clear that the States were retaining every power not delegated to the new government, the Tenth Amendment states, "The powers not delegated to the United States by the Constitution, nor prohibited by it to the States, are reserved to the States respectively, or to the people." It could not be much clearer!

Initial euphoria over the new Constitution saw majorities of Federalists get elected to the new Congress and State legislatures, along with George Washington as the first President. Next would be the election to President of John Adams, Washington's Vice-President, who defeated Thomas Jefferson by a razor thin margin of seventy-one electoral votes to sixty-eight. The minority Anti-Federalists, many who now called themselves Republican's, began to unite under the leadership of Thomas Jefferson who had become Vice-President.

The administration of John Adams and the Federalist Congress passed the Alien and Sedition Act's which expanded the powers of the Federal government un-constitutionally, thought the Republicans. The Sedition Act prohibited any criticism of the Executive or Legislative branches of the Federal government, with the exception of the Vice-President (Thomas Jefferson). The Alien Acts allowed the President to expel foreign persons "without jury, without public trial, without confrontation of the witnesses against him, without having witnesses in his favor, without defense, and without counsel" and denied persons their liberty without due process of law and their procedural rights under the Fifth and Sixth Amendments (McClellan, 492).

In response to these Acts, the States of Kentucky and Virginia would produce what would become to many the bedrock foundation of States Rights theory, the Kentucky and Virginia Resolutions or Resolutions of '98, written by Thomas Jefferson and James Madison. However, these Resolutions were not a novel idea. As Dr. Kevin Gutzman notes, "The Virginia and Kentucky Resolutions of 1798 should not be considered as the invention of distraught minds... the twin enunciations of the Republican constitutional   position adopted by the Virginia and Kentucky legislatures corresponded closely to the explication of the federal Constitution offered by Virginia Federalists in the Richmond Ratification Convention of 1788" (Gutzman, 114). The Resolves were a reminder that the States retained all power not delegated to the Federal government. Jefferson was only reiterating what the Federalists had conceded at the Federal and Virginia Ratification Conventions that the States retained all powers not delegated.

The first resolve of the Kentucky Resolution stated: "That the several States composing, the United States of America, are not united on the principle of unlimited submission to their general government; but that, by a compact under the style and title of a Constitution for the United States...they constituted a general government for special purposes — delegated to that government certain definite powers, reserving, each State to itself, the residuary mass of right to their own self-government...that the government created by this compact was not made the exclusive or final judge of the extent of the powers delegated to itself..." (Constitution Society). The Alien and Sedition Acts were the first notable attempt of the Federal Government to expand its powers in disregard of the bounds set by the Constitution. Jefferson and his fellow Republicans would win control of the Presidency and the Congress in the next election and Republicans would hold power for many years, effectively stemming the tide of the Federalists. However, many would still try to press on with a Nationalist agenda and it would take new leaders to fight back their advance, leaders like Judge St. George Tucker and John Taylor of Caroline.

States Rights Defended

St. George Tucker was a Virginian who studied law at the College of William and Mary and was admitted to the bar in 1775 at the age of twenty-three. He succeeded the famous George Wythe as Professor of Law at William and Mary in 1790 and was instrumental in updating Blackstones *Commentaries on the Laws of England* which was the preminent legal text of the era. Tucker's version included four volumes, which Clyde N. Wilson notes "for the first time brought the great chaotic mass of statutory and common law into a system that could be approached by students" (Tucker, viii). After the Revolution, Tucker needed to "republicanize Blackstone" in order to bring the law up to date with

American's new found way of Constitutional thinking "in which the people exercised their sovereign authority to create governments that rested specifically on the peoples consent..."(ibid, ix). Tucker included essays that appeared as appendices in the four volumes which then brought the total of volumes to five. The new five volume set of books was published in 1803 and was considered widely influential in the study of law until 1861 and the beginning of the War of Northern Aggression. In one of his essays entitled *View of the Constitution of the United States,* Tucker writes of the necessity for American students to "inquire into the connection established between the several states in the union by the constitution of the United States" (ibid, 91). He then goes on to explain the "nature of the document" and the manner in which it was adopted, its structure, organization, powers, jurisdiction and the rights of government thereby established. Tucker explains what type of government the Constitution established, "It is a Federal compact; several sovereign and independent states may unite themselves together by a perpetual confederacy, without each ceasing to be a perfect state. They will together form a federal republic." He goes on, "The extent, modifications, and objects of the federal authority are matters of discretion; so long as the separate organizations of the members remains, and from the nature of the compact must continue to exist, both for local and domestic, and for federal purposes; the union is in fact, as well as in theory, an association of states, or, a confederacy" (ibid, 92). Tucker understood as well as any legal mind of the era that the government created by the Framers, and established by the Ratifiers, was one of a confederacy of sovereign and independent States. To make it even more perfectly clear, he added, "The state governments not only retain every power, jurisdiction, and right not delegated to the

United States, by the constitution, nor prohibited by it to the states, but are constituent and necessary parts of the federal government..." (ibid, 92). Tucker goes on to explain that the Tenth Amendment to the Constitution[5] was added to "prevent misconstruction or abuse" of the powers granted by the constitution. This is taken straight from the preamble of the *Bill of Rights.*

John Taylor, also known as John Taylor of Caroline, was a lawyer, soldier, member of the Virginia House of Delegates and a United States Senator. He was a friend and supporter of Thomas Jefferson and sponsored James Madison's *Virginia Resolution* in the House of Delegates. He wrote extensively on the Constitution and its limited and delegated powers. He also wrote that "Sovereignty" was found neither in the Federal government or the State governments, but in the people of the several States. In one of the chapters of his book, *Construction Construed and Constitutions Vindicated,* Taylor inquired about the "Union." He asked; "Who made it? "We, the people, of the United States." But who are they? The associated inhabitants of each state, or the unassociated inhabitants of all the states" (Taylor, Construction Construed and Constitutions Vindicated, 39). He answered his own question by ascertaining the meaning of "we the people of the United States" by an examination of the constitutions of the different states:

• **New Hampshire**. The people of this state have the *sole and exclusive* right of governing themselves as a free, *sovereign* and independent *state.*

---

[5] Tucker, when writing his essays, refers to the Tenth Amendment as the "Twelfth Amendment" because at the time he wrote his lectures there were twelve proposed amendments.

- **Massachusetts**. The body politick is formed by voluntary *association of individuals*. The people of this commonwealth have the sole right of governing themselves as a free, *sovereign* and independent *state*.

- **New York**. This convention, in the name and by the authority of the good people of this state.

- **Pennsylvania**. We the people of the commonwealth of Pennsylvania ordain. The legislature of a free state.

- **Delaware**. The people of this state.

- **Maryland**. The people of this state ought to have sole and exclusive right of regulating the internal government thereof.

- **Virginia**. All power is derived from the people. Magistrates are their trustees or servants.

- **North Carolina**. The people of this state have the sole and exclusive right of regulating the internal government thereof.

- **Vermont**. The people are the sole source of power. They have the exclusive right of internal government. (ibid, 40-41)

It is clear by examining the wording from several of the State constitutions that "the people" meant the people of the individual States and not a consolidated nation made up of "one people." This fallacy has been perpetuated by many Historians, particularly Akhil Reed Amar in his book , *America's Constitution: A Biography* , in their attempt to promote an all-powerful central government at the expense of the States.

When discussing Article IV, section four, of the Constitution, which states "The United States shall guarantee to every State in this Union a Republican Form of Government…" Taylor notes that it was intended to secure the independence of each state, and not to subject each to a majority of the rest. Supposedly there was an argument by some that the guarantee of a republican form of government bestowed some "indistinct and unlimited national supremacy upon the federal government." Taylor explains to the contrary, "The word republican includes a right in the people of each state to form their own government; and reserves whatever other rights may be necessary to the exercise of this cardinal right. The right of the people in each state to create, and to influence their government, is the essential principle of a republican form of government, and therefore the guarantee could not have been intended as a means for destroying the essence of a republican form of government, by subjecting the people of every state to the arbitrary will of a federal majority, or to a majority of the supreme court" (Taylor, New Views of The Constitution, 227).

Over and over these facts are made clear by those who understood the true nature of the Constitution and the government it created. Sadly, these giants of their era, St. George Tucker and John Taylor, as well as the limited government espoused by them, have been almost forgotten by today's students of Law and History.

The Nationalist Cancer

It has been shown so far that the people of the individual States are the true sovereigns of the government. In their capacity as a people they have, since their arrival and settlement of this Continent, formed societies, communities,

Colonies and eventually States. There should be no question that the people formed governments that suited their way of life and held jealously to the right to alter or abolish those governments when they wished. The people of the several Colonies made treaties with each other, fought battles against one another, and ultimately formed a Union to protect their individual rights. The debates during the Federal Convention of 1787 have shown that many in attendance wanted to undue that long history and form a consolidated, National government, but were soundly defeated. When it came to the State ratifying conventions those who advocated for a much more powerful central government had to backtrack and convince the people that the new Constitution was adhering to a Federal theory of government and was granted only certain enumerated powers. The ascendency of Thomas Jefferson and the republicans seemed to be vindication of these principles. In an ironic twist, several Federalist controlled New England States would invoke the *Resolutions of '98*. In December of 1814 through January 1815, the New England States of Massachusetts, Connecticut, Rhode Island, Vermont and New Hampshire met at a convention in Hartford, Connecticut. The meeting, known as the Hartford Convention, was precipitated by the "policies of the Jeffersonian Republicans, the administration of James Madison and the War of 1812" (McClellan, 494-495). The convention delegates wanted amendments to the Constitution to correct problems which the Federalists believed, were deeply affecting their interest. If the problems were not corrected, these States threatened to secede from the Union. Even this New England bastion of Federalists understood that they could resume their powers at anytime. The doctrine of States right's had triumphed throughout the nation and the Federalists were reeling.

After Jefferson, the next several Presidents were all States rights adherents. Madison had forsaken his Nationalist tendencies of the Federal Convention and now championed the rights of the States. After Madison came James Monroe and then Andrew Jackson. John Quincy Adams, a one term President who leaned Federalist, was the only exception during this run.

However, like a cancer, the belief in an all-powerful central government was hard to destroy. Staunch Nationalist, like Chief Justice John Marshall, would find ways to undermine the authority of the States and create what his ilk so longed for, a Supreme National government. But there was one pesky problem that would stand in the way, the Tenth Amendment.

While John Marshall was indeed a Nationalist, even he had to concede that the *Bills of Rights* were intended as a check on the Federal government and not the States. In his *Baron v. Baltimore* (32 U.S. 243) decision, Marshall makes it quite clear, "But it is universally understood, it is a part of the history of the day, that the great revolution which established the Constitution of the United States was not effected without immense opposition. Serious fears were extensively entertained that those powers which the patriot statesmen who then watched over the interests of our country deemed essential to union, and to the attainment of those invaluable objects for which union was sought, might be exercised in a manner dangerous to liberty. In almost every convention by which the Constitution was adopted, amendments to guard against the abuse of power were recommended. *These amendments demanded security against the apprehended encroachments of the General Government -- not against those of the local governments.* In compliance with a sentiment thus generally expressed, to quiet fears thus extensively entertained, amendments were proposed by the required majority in Congress and adopted by the States. These amendments contain no expression indicating an intention to apply them to the State governments. This court cannot so apply them" (emphasis added).

While John Marshall, for the moment, remembered how and why the Constitution was framed and ratified, it was not long before he found more ways to expand the power of the Federal government. One decision after another by the Marshall Court granted the Federal government more and more power at the expense of the States. A new doctrine would be established that would have far reaching consequences on the relationship between the Federal government and the States that created it. As noted earlier, the Constitution had been ratified by the people of the individual States in their sovereign capacity, but now, Marshall would proclaim that the Constitution was created by the whole people, who for convenience sake, met in State conventions. This doctrine would ultimately take precedence over the truth and we suffer for it today. However, the States would not just roll over for Marshall and his minions on the Supreme Court. Time and again they would stand up to his unconstitutional dictates. One such instance was after the *M'Culloch v. Maryland* (17 U.S. 316) decision, a case that involved the controversial *Bank of the United States* and the States power of taxation. The landmark decision went against the States and immediately caused uproar. Several States simply refused to abide by the decision. In Ohio, the State auditor sent his assistant to the U.S. Bank and ordered him to remove from the vaults the tax owed to the State, by force if necessary. The assistant removed $120,000 in gold and notes and placed them in the State treasury in direct contempt of a Federal

Court order (Mc Donald, States Rights And The Union 1776-1876, 82). After a similar decision by the Supreme Court in *Osborn v. Bank of the United States* (22 U.S. 738), which was held by many to negate the Eleventh Amendment, the State of Kentucky enacted several laws that protected debtors. The legislation was deemed unconstitutional by the States lower courts and its court of Appeals. The legislature was so outraged at the court's decision that "It adopted a ringing resolution denouncing the court for overturning a solemn act of the sovereign state and declared its intention to disregard the ruling...the Kentucky legislature considered impeaching the judges of the court of appeals... then hit upon a different expedient. It abolished the court and created a new court of appeals (ibid, 83). However, the attack on the States continued, and new leaders would arise to defend their sovereignty. One such leader was John C. Calhoun of South Carolina. Calhoun was originally a Nationalist and served as Vice President to John Quincy Adams. However, as the economy soured, Northern leaders looked to protective tariffs as a means of supporting Northern Industry and Calhoun believed that the tariffs were unconstitutional. Once again the *Resolutions of '98* would come into play. Calhoun espoused a theory that would become known as interposition or "Nullification" in which the States would interpose their authority between the people and the Federal government in order to protect them against unconstitutional attacks. It was regarded as a step prior to secession that would hold the Union together. Even staunch Federalist like Daniel Webster agreed "that if Calhoun's analysis of the origin of the Constitution was sound, the doctrine of nullification was sound" (ibid, 109). South Carolina's legislature enacted a Nullifying Conventions ordinance that declared the tariffs of 1828 and 1832 "unconstitutional, null and void and forbade

the collection in the state of the duties leveled against them"
(South Carolina Ordinance of Nullification, November 24,
1832). Andrew Jackson was willing to send troops to enforce
the tariff but a showdown was averted when the tariffs were
significantly lowered and South Carolina rescinded its
Nullifying ordinance.

The doctrine espoused by John Marshall, that the Constitution
was formed by the people as a whole, was a troubling omen
for those who believed in the principle of the Union as a
compact between sovereign States, formed by sovereign
people. Over the next few decades the struggle would
continue back and forth, culminating in a showdown that
would cause the deaths of hundreds of thousands and change
forever the nature of the Union.

The War of Northern Aggression and its Aftermath

April 9, 1865 marked the beginning of the end for the Union
as envisioned by those that ratified the Constitution. On that
day Robert E. Lee surrendered the Army of Northern
Virginia, effectively ending the Southern Confederacy.
Trampled to death after nearly four years of warfare and
hundreds of thousands of deaths was the idea of consensual
government.

There are many theories for why the war was started, slavery,
tariffs, and the preservation of the union to name a few, but
only one really matters: Secession. The Southern States,
disregarding whether or not it was a smart choice, felt it
necessary to leave the Union and form a new confederation.
Similar to the thirteen colonies of 1776, they re-declared their
independence and followed the words of the Declaration of
Independence that stated " …that whenever and Form of
Government becomes destructive…it is the Right of the

People to alter or abolish it, and institute new government…
on such principles…that seem most likely to effect their
Safety and Happiness." After the war, Alexander Stephens
wrote a two volume treatise entitled *A Constitutional View of
the late War Between the States,* in which he defended the
right of secession. Stephens, who hailed from Georgia, served
in its House of Representatives and Senate, and served in the
United States Congress for more than a decade. When
Georgia seceded and the new Confederate government was
formed, he was picked as its Vice-President. Stephens was no
fire-breathing secessionist but a staunch defender of the
Union who, in 1851, was elected to Congress as a Union
Party member. His book was written as a colloquy between
himself and three Gentlemen (which according to Stephens
were given three fictitious names to protect their identity)
representing a Massachusetts Radical Republican, a
Connecticut Conservative and a Pennsylvania War Democrat.
In the first chapter the Radical Republican states: "We were
all at the North very much surprised as well as disappointed,
Mr. Stephens, at your course on Secession." When asked,
why? by Stephens, the Radical spoke of a speech that
Stephens delivered in the Georgia Legislature on November
14th, 1860, that was considered "as one of the best Union
speeches ever made." Stephens then went on to concede that
"No stronger or more ardent Union man ever lived than was
I", but then asked, "But what Union? or the Union of what?"
(Stephens, 18). Stephens then went on to say that he was
ardently devoted to the Union of States under the
Constitution, not a Union that was considered by those in the
North, to mean the unity of the whole people of the United
States, as one nation. He explained, "Well, allow me to say
that there never was in this country any such union as you
speak of; there never was a political union between the people

61

of the several States of the United States, except such as resulted indirectly from the terms of agreement or Compact entered into by separate and distinct political bodies" (ibid, 19). The Radical Republican was echoing the doctrine of John Marshall and Stephens replied with the doctrine of the Founding Fathers.

The President of the Confederacy was also a man who had whole-heartedly supported the Union, Jefferson Davis. Davis, from Mississippi, was a graduate of West Point, served in the war with Mexico, was a United States Senator and Secretary of War under Franklin Pierce. He was also a staunch supporter of States' Rights who tendered his resignation from the United States Senate when Mississippi seceded from the Union. The speech he gave from the Senate floor on January 21, 1861 was impassioned and described the difference between what John C. Calhoun once advocated, nullification and the ultimate act of secession. He spoke thus: "A great man who now reposes with his fathers, and who has often been arraigned for want of fealty to the Union, advocated the doctrine of nullification because it preserved the Union. It was because of his deep-seated attachment to the Union—his determination to find some remedy for existing ills short of a severance of the ties which bound South Carolina to the other States—that Mr. Calhoun advocated the doctrine of nullification, which he proclaimed to be peaceful, to be within the limits of State power, not to disturb the Union, but only to be a means of bringing the agent before the tribunal of the States for their judgment. Secession belongs to a different class of remedies. It is to be justified upon the basis that the states are sovereign. There was a time when none denied it. I hope the time may come again when a better comprehension of the theory of our Government, and the inalienable rights of the people of the States, will prevent anyone from denying that each State is a sovereign, and thus may reclaim the grants which it has made to any agent whomsoever" (History.org, Calhoun Speech 2011).

These Southern leaders understood that the people of the Sovereign states had entered the Union voluntarily and could withdraw from it voluntarily. Davis and Stephens were not claiming anything new. Their statements harkened back to the ratification documents of States such as New York and Virginia, Rhode Island and Massachusetts. Whether or not secession was a smart or practical idea is moot. Acting in their sovereign capacity the people of the Southern States chose to leave a Union that they believed was no longer beneficial or conducive to their well being. It was their right to do so, and they proceeded in a peaceful manner. Davis finished, "I am sure I feel no hostility toward you, Senators from the North. I am sure there is not one of you, whatever sharp discussion there may have been between us, to whom I cannot now say, in the presence of my God, I wish you well; and such, I feel, is the feeling of the people whom I represent toward those whom you represent. I, therefore, feel that I but express their desire when I say I hope, and they hope, for peaceable relations with you, though we must part" (ibid).

In comparison, Abraham Lincoln, a believer in the Marshall doctrine of a consolidated people, initiated and pursued a destructive war against a people who only wished to govern themselves as their forefathers did. In his inaugural address Lincoln perpetuates the myth of a perpetual and consolidated Union, "...the Union is perpetual, confirmed by the history of the Union itself. The Union is much older than the Constitution" (Wills, 130-131). What Union was Lincoln talking about? The only Union that ever existed was one of

Independent States whose people repeatedly commissioned delegates to act on their behalf, whether it was for the Continental Congress, the Confederation formed by the Articles of Confederation or the Federal Constitution. New York's Constitution of 1777 made it quite clear that there was no "Nation" as yet and contained these words (Emphasis added):

" 'Resolved, That it be recommended to the respective assemblies and conventions of the United colonies, *where no government sufficient to the exigencies of their affairs has been hitherto established, to adopt such government as shall, in the opinion of the representatives of the people, best conduce to the happiness and safety of their constituents in particular, and America in general.'*

"And whereas doubts have arisen whether this congress are invested with sufficient power and authority to deliberate and determine on so important a subject as the necessity of erecting and constituting a new form of government and internal police, to the exclusion of all foreign jurisdiction, dominion, and control whatever; *and whereas it appertains of right solely to the people of this colony to determine the said doubts...*

I.	This convention, therefore, in the name and by the authority of the good people of this State, doth ordain, determine, and declare *that no authority shall, on any presence whatever, be exercised over the people or members of this State but such as shall be derived from and granted by them.*

It is quite clear that New Yorker's understood that there was no "government" or "Nation" established at the time and that it was "solely to the people of this colony" to determine if there even should be one!

Even Lincoln's Gettysburg address is a farce. "Fourscore and seven years ago our forefathers brought forth…a new nation…dedicated to the proposition that all men are created equal." What Nation is he speaking of that was "brought forth"? The Declaration of Independence states "all men are created equal" but what "nation" did the Declaration bring forth? The Declaration, remember, was the States declaring themselves to be "Free and Independent" from the tyrannical rule of a centralized government, not a nation. The Articles of Confederation never declared that "all men are created equal" and it was a styled a Confederation with each state retaining its sovereignty, freedom and independence. The Union formed under the then current Constitution never claimed equality for anyone. Lincoln's assertion that "the government of the people, by the people, and for the people, shall not perish from the earth" was a lie. At the time of the speech, Lincoln was doing all in his power to destroy the right of a people to live as they saw fit in contravention of every notion of liberty that existed from the first English settlement of the continent.

With the fall of the Confederacy, Lincoln and his minions, for all intent and purposes, accomplished at the point of bayonet the consolidation of the Union and the annihilation of the sovereignty of the people of the individual States.

After the war and a horrible reconstruction period, the States of the South began a long and arduous journey back into the Union they had fought so valiantly, and sacrificed so much, to leave. Nothing beneficial had changed since the events that precipitated them to leave years earlier, in fact it was worse. The Confederation that was born in Liberty and baptized in blood at places like Lexington and Concord, Bunker Hill, Saratoga, and Yorktown, had ceased to exist. The people were no longer allowed to choose for themselves the type of government they felt best suited their needs. The Declaration of Independence, while outwardly honored, was a mere parchment of words "full of sound and fury, signifying nothing." The government no longer truly derived its rights from the consent of the governed, it became a new Master. Woe to anyone who ever again wished to change or abolish it.

Summary

The Constitution has been ignored by an all-powerful, central government that has exceeded the wildest dreams of Alexander Hamilton. King George of England never had the power that the "Federal" government has today. The President of the United States can arbitrarily commit the young men and women of the several States to any foreign war or intervention he chooses without a peep from a Congress who constitutionally has the sole power to declare war. The Federal government through Presidential decrees, acts of Congress and edicts from the Supreme Court, can seize your firearms (BATF), prohibit your religious practices (*Engel V. Vitale 370 U.S. 421* 1962), deny your right to free speech (*Schenck V. United States 249 U.S. 47* 1919), seize your income and property (IRS), tell you what you can and cannot eat (FDA) and intrude in almost every aspect of your life and you are powerless to stop it. Try and you will be imprisoned or worse, murdered by Federal agents empowered to act on the Governments behalf. There have been attempts over the years by the States to reassert their sovereignty, but they came to naught.

Today, the doctrine of a consolidated Union is considered as written in stone. Scholars and Lawyers will proclaim that the Fourteenth Amendment has "Incorporated" the Bill of Rights as a check against the States and a means for the Federal government to have jurisdiction inside the States in total disregard of the Constitution and the Founders intent. Raoul Berger, a law professor at the University of California, Berkeley, and a Charles Warren Senior Fellow in American Legal History at Harvard Law School did extensive research on the Fourteenth Amendment. In his book *Government by Judiciary: the Transformation of the Fourteenth Amendment*, he writes "The architect of the "incorporation" theory, Justice (Hugo) Black, invoked some fragmentary history-utterances in connection with an explanation of "privileges or immunities" by two leading Republicans..." he continued, "The words "privileges and immunities" seemed "an eminently reasonable way of expressing the idea that henceforth the Bill of Rights shall apply to the States" (Berger, 157- 159). Berger then goes on to explain the original idea of "privileges or immunities" which "...had its roots in Article IV, section 2, which requires States to accord certain privileges to citizens of a sister State, the Bill of Rights, on the other hand, was designed to protect certain rights *against* the federal government" (ibid, 159 Emphasis added). Also, according to Berger, no one in the 39th Congress, the Congress that ratified the Fourteenth Amendment, intimated that the "due process" clause would incorporate the Bill of Rights as many proclaim today. The Supreme Court would continually rule against the States and further erode the idea of a Confederation based on a voluntary association amongst equals.

How did we allow this to happen? For starters, we have

forgotten that the true foundation of our freedom begins with "We, the people of the States." We listen to the "Scholars" and Lawyers who tell us the Federal government is all-powerful and accept it as Gospel. Powers that were never delegated to the Federal government are routinely used to gain access to every aspect of our lives. State Governors and Legislatures, who once stood tall against unconstitutional usurpation of power, now kowtow to the Federal government, begging for handouts and groveling at the feet of their new master. We should be ashamed of ourselves.

It is the purpose of this paper to examine the original relationship between the Federal and State governments and the true nature of our Federal form of government. I have documented how, since the earliest settlement of the Continent, the people held jealously the right to govern themselves and eventually fought a long bloody war to establish that principle. For generations, the people knew that their local government was the protector of their liberties and when change was needed, it could be affected on a local level by representatives who were elected by them and lived amongst them. If we are to regain our lost liberty, to live as we choose and restore the Constitution of our Forefathers, we will need to understand that we, the people, hold the power, not the Federal government.

We are a unique people with different ideologies and prejudices, who created the political entities called States because we wanted to live amongst people who thought and acted like ourselves. These States are the places we call home, where our attachments lie. There we raise our families, work, play, establish friendships, retire, and grow old with our memories. We have been taught to ignore that attachment and to regard the whole United States as our home, but this diminishes who we really are; New Yorkers, Virginians, Georgians etc…

We should take heed from those Patriots of old, who committed their lives in the pursuit of freedom and liberty, and who after much suffering, depredation and death, gave us a chance to live free and pursue our dreams. They fought hard to assure that the government that was being created was one of limited authority and that the "The powers not delegated to the United States by the Constitution, nor prohibited by it to the States, are reserved to the States respectively, or to the people." Have we been worthy of the sacrifices made by so many? Are we still free?

"The liberties of our Country, the freedom of our civil constitution are worth defending at all hazards: And it is our duty to defend them against all attacks. We have receiv'd them as a fair Inheritance from our worthy Ancestors: They purchas'd them for us with toil and danger and expense of treasure and blood; and transmitted them to us with care and diligence. It will bring an everlasting mark of infamy on the present generation, enlightened as it is, if we should suffer them to be wrested from us by violence without a struggle; or be cheated out of them by the artifices of false and designing men. Of the latter we are in most danger at present: Let us therefore be aware of it. Let us contemplate our forefathers and posterity; and resolve to maintain the rights bequeath'd to us from the former, for the sake of the latter. - Instead of sitting down satisfied with the efforts we have already made, which is the wish of our enemies, the necessity of the times, more than ever, calls for our utmost circumspection, deliberation, fortitude, and perseverance. Let us remember that "if we suffer tamely a lawless attack upon our liberty, we encourage it, and involve others in our doom." It is a very serious consideration, which should deeply impress our minds, that millions yet unborn may be the miserable sharers of the event." - Samuel Adams Essay in the Boston Gazette, October 14, 1771

The Constitution of the United States

Preamble

We the People of the United States, in Order to form a more perfect Union, establish Justice, insure domestic Tranquility, provide for the common defense, promote the general Welfare, and secure the Blessings of Liberty to ourselves and our Posterity, do ordain and establish this Constitution for the United States of America.

Article I - The Legislative Branch

Section 1 - The Legislature

All legislative Powers herein granted shall be vested in a Congress of the United States, which shall consist of a Senate and House of Representatives.

Section 2 - The House

The House of Representatives shall be composed of Members chosen every second Year by the People of the several States, and the Electors in each State shall have the Qualifications requisite for Electors of the most numerous Branch of the State Legislature.

No Person shall be a Representative who shall not have attained to the Age of twenty five Years, and been seven Years a Citizen of the United States, and who shall not, when elected, be an Inhabitant of that State in which he shall be chosen.

(Representatives and direct Taxes shall be apportioned among the several States which may be included within this

Union, according to their respective Numbers, which shall be determined by adding to the whole Number of free Persons, including those bound to Service for a Term of Years, and excluding Indians not taxed, three fifths of all other Persons.) **(The previous sentence in parentheses was modified by the 14th Amendment, section 2.)**

The actual Enumeration shall be made within three Years after the first Meeting of the Congress of the United States, and within every subsequent Term of ten Years, in such Manner as they shall by Law direct. The Number of Representatives shall not exceed one for every thirty Thousand, but each State shall have at Least one Representative; and until such enumeration shall be made, the State of New Hampshire shall be entitled to chuse three, Massachusetts eight, Rhode Island and Providence Plantations one, Connecticut five, New York six, New Jersey four, Pennsylvania eight, Delaware one, Maryland six, Virginia ten, North Carolina five, South Carolina five and Georgia three.

When vacancies happen in the Representation from any State, the Executive Authority thereof shall issue Writs of Election to fill such Vacancies.

The House of Representatives shall chuse their Speaker and other Officers; and shall have the sole Power of Impeachment.

Section 3 - The Senate

The Senate of the United States shall be composed of two Senators from each State,*(chosen by the Legislature thereof,)* **(The preceding words in parentheses superseded by 17th**

Amendment, section 1.) for six Years; and each Senator shall have one Vote.

Immediately after they shall be assembled in Consequence of the first Election, they shall be divided as equally as may be into three Classes. The Seats of the Senators of the first Class shall be vacated at the Expiration of the second Year, of the second Class at the Expiration of the fourth Year, and of the third Class at the Expiration of the sixth Year, so that one third may be chosen every second Year;*(and if Vacancies happen by Resignation, or otherwise, during the Recess of the Legislature of any State, the Executive thereof may make temporary Appointments until the next Meeting of the Legislature, which shall then fill such Vacancies.)* **(The preceding words in parentheses were superseded by the 17th Amendment, section 2.)**

No person shall be a Senator who shall not have attained to the Age of thirty Years, and been nine Years a Citizen of the United States, and who shall not, when elected, be an Inhabitant of that State for which he shall be chosen.

The Vice President of the United States shall be President of the Senate, but shall have no Vote, unless they be equally divided.

The Senate shall chuse their other Officers, and also a President pro tempore, in the absence of the Vice President, or when he shall exercise the Office of President of the United States.

The Senate shall have the sole Power to try all Impeachments. When sitting for that Purpose, they shall be on Oath or Affirmation. When the President of the United States is tried, the Chief Justice shall preside: And no Person shall be convicted without the Concurrence of two thirds of the Members present.

Judgment in Cases of Impeachment shall not extend further than to removal from Office, and disqualification to hold and enjoy any Office of honor, Trust or Profit under the United States: but the Party convicted shall nevertheless be liable and subject to Indictment, Trial, Judgment and Punishment, according to Law.

Section 4 - Elections, Meetings

The Times, Places and Manner of holding Elections for Senators and Representatives, shall be prescribed in each State by the Legislature thereof; but the Congress may at any time by Law make or alter such Regulations, except as to the Place of Chusing Senators.

The Congress shall assemble at least once in every Year, and such Meeting shall *(be on the first Monday in December,)* **(The preceding words in parentheses were superseded by the 20th Amendment, section 2.)** unless they shall by Law appoint a different Day.

Section 5 - Membership, Rules, Journals, Each House shall be the Judge of the Elections, Returns and Qualifications of its own Members, and a Majority of each shall constitute a Quorum to do Business; but a smaller number may adjourn from day to day, and may be authorized to compel the Attendance of absent Members, in such Manner, and under such Penalties as each House may provide.

Each House may determine the Rules of its Proceedings, punish its Members for disorderly Behavior, and, with the Concurrence of two-thirds, expel a Member.

Each House shall keep a Journal of its Proceedings, and from time to time publish the same, excepting such Parts as may in their Judgment require Secrecy; and the Yeas and Nays of the Members of either House on any question shall, at the Desire of one fifth of those Present, be entered on the Journal.

Neither House, during the Session of Congress, shall, without the Consent of the other, adjourn for more than three days, nor to any other Place than that in which the two Houses shall be sitting.

Section 6 - Compensation

(The Senators and Representatives shall receive a Compensation for their Services, to be ascertained by Law, and paid out of the Treasury of the United States.) **(The preceding words in parentheses were modified by the 27th Amendment.)**

They shall in all Cases, except Treason, Felony and Breach of the Peace, be privileged from Arrest during their Attendance at the Session of their respective Houses, and in going to and returning from the same; and for any Speech or Debate in either House, they shall not be questioned in any other Place.

No Senator or Representative shall, during the Time for which he was elected, be appointed to any civil Office under the Authority of the United States which shall have been created, or the Emoluments whereof shall have been increased during such time; and no Person holding any Office under the United States, shall be a Member of either House during his Continuance in Office.

Section 7 - Revenue Bills, Legislative Process, Presidential Veto

All bills for raising Revenue shall originate in the House of Representatives; but the Senate may propose or concur with Amendments as on other Bills.

Every Bill which shall have passed the House of Representatives and the Senate, shall, before it become a Law, be presented to the President of the United States; If he approve he shall sign it, but if not he shall return it, with his Objections to that House in which it shall have originated, who shall enter the Objections at large on their Journal, and proceed to reconsider it. If after such Reconsideration two thirds of that House shall agree to pass the Bill, it shall be sent, together with the Objections, to the other House, by which it shall likewise be reconsidered, and if approved by two thirds of that House, it shall become a Law. But in all such Cases the Votes of both Houses shall be determined by Yeas and Nays, and the Names of the Persons voting for and against the Bill shall be entered on the Journal of each House respectively. If any Bill shall not be returned by the President within ten Days (Sundays excepted) after it shall have been presented to him, the Same shall be a Law, in like Manner as if he had signed it, unless the Congress by their Adjournment prevent its Return, in which Case it shall not be a Law.

Every Order, Resolution, or Vote to which the Concurrence of the Senate and House of Representatives may be necessary (except on a question of Adjournment) shall be presented to the President of the United States; and before the Same shall take Effect, shall be approved by him, or being disapproved by him, shall be repassed by two thirds of the Senate and House of Representatives, according to the Rules and Limitations prescribed in the Case of a Bill.

Section 8 - Powers of Congress

The Congress shall have Power To lay and collect Taxes, Duties, <u>Imposts</u> and <u>Excises</u>, to pay the Debts and provide for the common Defense and general <u>Welfare</u> of the United States; but all Duties, <u>Imposts</u> and <u>Excises</u> shall be uniform throughout the United States;

To borrow money on the credit of the United States;

To regulate Commerce with foreign Nations, and among the several States, and with the Indian Tribes;

To establish an uniform Rule of Naturalization, and uniform Laws on the subject of Bankruptcies throughout the United States;

To coin Money, regulate the Value thereof, and of foreign Coin, and fix the Standard of Weights and Measures;

To provide for the Punishment of counterfeiting the Securities and current Coin of the United States;

To establish Post Offices and <u>Post Roads</u>;

To promote the Progress of Science and useful Arts, by securing for limited Times to Authors and Inventors the exclusive Right to their respective Writings and Discoveries;

To constitute Tribunals inferior to the supreme Court;

To define and punish Piracies and Felonies committed on the high Seas, and Offenses against the Law of Nations;

To declare War, grant Letters of Marque and Reprisal, and make Rules concerning Captures on Land and Water;

To raise and support Armies, but no Appropriation of Money to that Use shall be for a longer Term than two Years;

To provide and maintain a Navy;

To make Rules for the Government and Regulation of the land and naval Forces;

To provide for calling forth the Militia to execute the Laws of the Union, suppress Insurrections and repel Invasions;

To provide for organizing, arming, and disciplining, the Militia, and for governing such Part of them as may be employed in the Service of the United States, reserving to the States respectively, the Appointment of the Officers, and the Authority of training the Militia according to the discipline prescribed by Congress;

To exercise exclusive Legislation in all Cases whatsoever, over such District (not exceeding ten Miles square) as may, by Cession of particular States, and the acceptance of Congress, become the Seat of the Government of the United States, and to exercise like Authority over all Places purchased by the Consent of the Legislature of the State in which the Same shall be, for the Erection of Forts, Magazines, Arsenals, dock-Yards, and other needful Buildings; And

To make all Laws which shall be necessary and proper for carrying into Execution the foregoing Powers, and all other Powers vested by this Constitution in the Government of the United States, or in any Department or Officer thereof.

Section 9 - Limits on Congress

The Migration or Importation of such Persons as any of the States now existing shall think proper to admit, shall not be prohibited by the Congress prior to the Year one thousand eight hundred and eight, but a tax or duty may be imposed on such Importation, not exceeding ten dollars for each Person.

The privilege of the Writ of Habeas Corpus shall not be suspended, unless when in Cases of Rebellion or Invasion the public Safety may require it.

No Bill of Attainder or ex post facto Law shall be passed.

(No capitation, or other direct, Tax shall be laid, unless in Proportion to the Census or Enumeration herein before directed to be taken.) **(Section in parentheses clarified by the 16th Amendment.)**

No Tax or Duty shall be laid on Articles exported from any State.

No Preference shall be given by any Regulation of Commerce or Revenue to the Ports of one State over those of another: nor shall Vessels bound to, or from, one State, be obliged to enter, clear, or pay Duties in another.

No Money shall be drawn from the Treasury, but in Consequence of Appropriations made by Law; and a regular Statement and Account of the Receipts and Expenditures of all public Money shall be published from time to time.

No Title of Nobility shall be granted by the United States: And no Person holding any Office of Profit or Trust under them, shall, without the Consent of the Congress, accept of any present, Emolument, Office, or Title, of any kind whatever, from any King, Prince or foreign State.

Section 10 - Powers prohibited of States

No State shall enter into any Treaty, Alliance, or Confederation; grant Letters of Marque and Reprisal; coin

Money; emit <u>Bills of Credit</u>; make any Thing but gold and silver Coin a Tender in Payment of Debts; pass any Bill of <u>Attainder</u>, <u>ex post facto</u> Law, or Law impairing the Obligation of Contracts, or grant any <u>Title of Nobility</u>.

No State shall, without the Consent of the Congress, lay any <u>Imposts</u> or Duties on Imports or Exports, except what may be absolutely necessary for executing <u>it's</u> inspection Laws: and the net Produce of all Duties and <u>Imposts</u>, laid by any State on Imports or Exports, shall be for the Use of the Treasury of the United States; and all such Laws shall be subject to the Revision and <u>Controul</u> of the Congress.

No State shall, without the Consent of Congress, lay any duty of Tonnage, keep Troops, or Ships of War in time of Peace, enter into any Agreement or Compact with another State, or with a foreign Power, or engage in War, unless actually invaded, or in such imminent Danger as will not admit of delay.

Article II - The Executive Branch

Section 1 - The President

The executive Power shall be vested in a President of the United States of America. He shall hold his Office during the Term of four Years, and, together with the Vice-President chosen for the same Term, be elected, as follows:

Each State shall appoint, in such Manner as the Legislature thereof may direct, a Number of Electors, equal to the whole Number of Senators and Representatives to which the State may be entitled in the Congress: but no Senator or Representative, or Person holding an Office of Trust or Profit under the United States, shall be appointed an Elector.

(The Electors shall meet in their respective States, and vote by Ballot for two persons, of whom one at least shall not lie an Inhabitant of the same State with themselves. And they shall make a List of all the Persons voted for, and of the Number of Votes for each; which List they shall sign and certify, and transmit sealed to the Seat of the Government of the United States, directed to the President of the Senate. The President of the Senate shall, in the Presence of the Senate and House of Representatives, open all the Certificates, and the Votes shall then be counted. The Person having the greatest Number of Votes shall be the President, if such Number be a Majority of the whole Number of Electors appointed; and if there be more than one who have such Majority, and have an equal Number of Votes, then the House of Representatives shall immediately chuse by Ballot one of them for President; and if no Person have a Majority, then from the five highest on the List the said House shall in like Manner chuse the President. But in chusing the President, the Votes shall be taken by States, the Representation from each State having one Vote; a quorum for this Purpose shall consist of a Member or Members from two-thirds of the States, and a Majority of all the States shall be necessary to a Choice. In every Case, after the Choice of the President, the Person having the greatest Number of Votes of the Electors shall be the Vice President. But if there should remain two or more who have equal Votes, the Senate shall chuse from them by Ballot the Vice-President.) **(This clause in parentheses was superseded by the 12th Amendment.)**

The Congress may determine the Time of chusing the Electors, and the Day on which they shall give their Votes; which Day shall be the same throughout the United States.

No person except a natural born Citizen, or a Citizen of the United States, at the time of the Adoption of this Constitution, shall be eligible to the Office of President; neither shall any Person be eligible to that Office who shall not have attained to the Age of thirty-five Years, and been fourteen Years a Resident within the United States.

(In Case of the Removal of the President from Office, or of his Death, Resignation, or Inability to discharge the Powers and Duties of the said Office, the same shall devolve on the Vice President, and the Congress may by Law provide for the Case of Removal, Death, Resignation or Inability, both of the President and Vice President, declaring what Officer shall then act as President, and such Officer shall act accordingly, until the Disability be removed, or a President shall be elected.) **(This clause in parentheses has been modified by the 20th and 25th Amendments.)**

The President shall, at stated Times, receive for his Services, a Compensation, which shall neither be increased nor diminished during the Period for which he shall have been elected, and he shall not receive within that Period any other Emolument from the United States, or any of them.

Before he enter on the Execution of his Office, he shall take the following Oath or Affirmation:

"I do solemnly swear (or affirm) that I will faithfully execute the Office of President of the United States, and will to the best of my Ability, preserve, protect and defend the Constitution of the United States."

Section 2 - Civilian Power over Military, Cabinet, Pardon Power, Appointments

The President shall be Commander in Chief of the Army and Navy of the United States, and of the Militia of the several States, when called into the actual Service of the United States; he may require the Opinion, in writing, of the principal Officer in each of the executive Departments, upon any subject relating to the Duties of their respective Offices, and he shall have Power to Grant Reprieves and Pardons for Offenses against the United States, except in Cases of Impeachment.

He shall have Power, by and with the Advice and Consent of the Senate, to make Treaties, provided two thirds of the Senators present concur; and he shall nominate, and by and with the Advice and Consent of the Senate, shall appoint Ambassadors, other public Ministers and Consuls, Judges of the supreme Court, and all other Officers of the United States, whose Appointments are not herein otherwise provided for, and which shall be established by Law: but the Congress may by Law vest the Appointment of such inferior Officers, as they think proper, in the President alone, in the Courts of Law, or in the Heads of Departments.

The President shall have Power to fill up all Vacancies that may happen during the Recess of the Senate, by granting Commissions which shall expire at the End of their next Session.

Section 3 - State of the Union, Convening Congress

He shall from time to time give to the Congress Information of the State of the Union, and recommend to their Consideration such Measures as he shall judge necessary and expedient; he may, on extraordinary Occasions, convene both Houses, or either of them, and in Case of Disagreement between them, with Respect to the Time of Adjournment, he may adjourn them to such Time as he shall think proper; he shall receive Ambassadors and other public Ministers; he shall take Care that the Laws be faithfully executed, and shall Commission all the Officers of the United States.

Section 4 - Disqualification

The President, Vice President and all civil Officers of the United States, shall be removed from Office on Impeachment for, and Conviction of, Treason, Bribery, or other high Crimes and Misdemeanors.

Article III - The Judicial Branch

Section 1 - Judicial powers

The judicial Power of the United States, shall be vested in one supreme Court, and in such inferior Courts as the Congress may from time to time ordain and establish. The Judges, both of the supreme and inferior Courts, shall hold their Offices during good Behavior, and shall, at stated Times, receive for their Services a Compensation which shall not be diminished during their Continuance in Office.

Section 2 - Trial by Jury, Original Jurisdiction, Jury Trials

(The judicial Power shall extend to all Cases, in Law and Equity, arising under this Constitution, the Laws of the United States, and Treaties made, or which shall be made, under their Authority; to all Cases affecting Ambassadors, other public Ministers and Consuls; to all Cases of admiralty and maritime Jurisdiction; to Controversies to which the United States shall be a Party; to Controversies between two

or more States; between a State and Citizens of another State; between Citizens of different States; between Citizens of the same State claiming Lands under Grants of different States, and between a State, or the Citizens thereof, and foreign States, Citizens or Subjects.) **(This section in parentheses is modified by the <u>11th Amendment</u>.)**

In all Cases affecting Ambassadors, other public Ministers and Consuls, and those in which a State shall be Party, the supreme Court shall have original <u>Jurisdiction</u>. In all the other Cases before mentioned, the supreme Court shall have <u>appellate</u> <u>Jurisdiction</u>, both as to Law and Fact, with such Exceptions, and under such Regulations as the Congress shall make.

The Trial of all Crimes, except in Cases of <u>Impeachment</u>, shall be by Jury; and such Trial shall be held in the State where the said Crimes shall have been committed; but when not committed within any State, the Trial shall be at such Place or Places as the Congress may by Law have directed.

Section 3 – Treason

<u>Treason</u> against the United States, shall consist only in levying War against them, or in adhering to their Enemies, giving them Aid and Comfort. No Person shall be convicted of <u>Treason</u> unless on the Testimony of two Witnesses to the same overt Act, or on Confession in open Court.

The Congress shall have power to declare the Punishment of <u>Treason</u>, but no Attainder of <u>Treason</u> shall work <u>Corruption of Blood</u>, or Forfeiture except during the Life of the Person attainted.

Article IV - The States

Section 1 - Each State to Honor all others

Full Faith and Credit shall be given in each State to the public Acts, Records, and judicial Proceedings of every other State. And the Congress may by general Laws prescribe the Manner in which such Acts, Records and Proceedings shall be proved, and the Effect thereof.

Section 2 - State citizens, Extradition

The Citizens of each State shall be entitled to all Privileges and Immunities of Citizens in the several States.

A Person charged in any State with <u>Treason</u>, Felony, or other Crime, who shall flee from Justice, and be found in another State, shall on demand of the executive Authority of the State from which he fled, be delivered up, to be removed to the State having <u>Jurisdiction</u> of the Crime.

(No Person held to Service or <u>Labour</u> in one State, under the Laws thereof, escaping into another, shall, in Consequence of any Law or Regulation therein, be discharged from such Service or <u>Labour</u>, But shall be delivered up on Claim of the Party to whom such Service or <u>Labour</u> may be due.) **(This clause in parentheses is superseded by the <u>13th Amendment</u>.)**

Section 3 - New States

New States may be admitted by the Congress into this Union; but no new States shall be formed or erected within the <u>Jurisdiction</u> of any other State; nor any State be formed by the Junction of two or more States, or parts of States, without the Consent of the Legislatures of the States concerned as well as of the Congress.

The Congress shall have Power to dispose of and make all needful Rules and Regulations respecting the Territory or other Property belonging to the United States; and nothing in this Constitution shall be so construed as to Prejudice any Claims of the United States, or of any particular State.

Section 4 - Republican government

The United States shall guarantee to every State in this Union a <u>Republican</u> Form of Government, and shall protect each of them against Invasion; and on Application of the Legislature, or of the Executive (when the Legislature cannot be convened) against domestic Violence.

Article V - Amendment

The Congress, whenever two thirds of both Houses shall deem it necessary, shall propose Amendments to this Constitution, or, on the Application of the Legislatures of two thirds of the several States, shall call a Convention for proposing Amendments, which, in either Case, shall be valid to all Intents and Purposes, as part of this Constitution, when ratified by the Legislatures of three fourths of the several States, or by Conventions in three fourths thereof, as the one or the other Mode of Ratification may be proposed by the Congress; Provided that no Amendment which may be made prior to the Year One thousand eight hundred and eight shall in any Manner affect the first and fourth Clauses in the Ninth Section of the first Article; and that no State, without its Consent, shall be <u>deprived</u> of its equal Suffrage in the Senate.

Article VI - Debts, Supremacy, Oaths

All Debts contracted and Engagements entered into, before the Adoption of this Constitution, shall be as valid against the United States under this Constitution, as under the Confederation.

This Constitution, and the Laws of the United States which shall be made in Pursuance thereof; and all Treaties made, or which shall be made, under the Authority of the United States, shall be the supreme Law of the Land; and the Judges in every State shall be bound thereby, any Thing in the Constitution or Laws of any State to the Contrary notwithstanding.

The Senators and Representatives before mentioned, and the Members of the several State Legislatures, and all executive and judicial Officers, both of the United States and of the several States, shall be bound by Oath or Affirmation, to support this Constitution; but no religious Test shall ever be required as a Qualification to any Office or public Trust under the United States.

Article VII - Ratification

The Ratification of the Conventions of nine States, shall be sufficient for the Establishment of this Constitution between the States so ratifying the Same.

Done in Convention by the Unanimous Consent of the States present the Seventeenth Day of September in the Year of our Lord one thousand seven hundred and Eighty seven and of the Independence of the United States of America the Twelfth. In Witness whereof We have hereunto subscribed our Names.

Go Washington - President and deputy from Virginia

New Hampshire - John Langdon, Nicholas Gilman

Massachusetts - Nathaniel Gorham, Rufus King

Connecticut - Wm Saml Johnson, Roger Sherman

New York - Alexander Hamilton

New Jersey - Wil Livingston, David Brearley, Wm Paterson, Jona. Dayton

Pennsylvania - B Franklin, Thomas Mifflin, Robt Morris, Geo. Clymer, Thos FitzSimons, Jared Ingersoll, James Wilson, Gouv Morris

Delaware - Geo. Read, Gunning Bedford jun, John Dickinson, Richard Bassett, Jaco. Broom

Maryland - James McHenry, Dan of St Tho Jenifer, Danl Carroll

Virginia - John Blair, James Madison Jr.

North Carolina - Wm Blount, Richd Dobbs Spaight, Hu Williamson

South Carolina - J. Rutledge, Charles Cotesworth Pinckney, Charles Pinckney, Pierce Butler

Georgia - William Few, Abr Baldwin

Attest: William Jackson, Secretary

Congress OF THE United States

begun and held at the City of New York, on Wednesday the Fourth of March, one thousand seven hundred and eighty nine.

THE Conventions of a number of the States having at the time of their adopting the Constitution, expressed a desire, in order to prevent misconstruction or abuse of its powers, that further declaratory and restrictive clauses should be added: And as extending the ground of public confidence in the Government, will best insure the beneficent ends of its institution

RESOLVED by the Senate and House of Representatives of the United States of America, in Congress assembled, two thirds of both Houses concurring, that the following Articles be proposed to the Legislatures of the several States, as Amendments to the Constitution of the United States, all or any of which Articles, when ratified by three fourths of the said Legislatures, to be valid to all intents and purposes, as part of the said Constitution; viz.:

ARTICLES in addition to, and Amendment of the Constitution of the United States of America, proposed by Congress, and ratified by the Legislatures of the several States, pursuant to the fifth Article of the original Constitution.

Amendment 1 - Freedom of Religion, Press, Expression. Ratified 12/15/1791.

Congress shall make no law respecting an establishment of religion, or prohibiting the free exercise thereof; or abridging the freedom of speech, or of the press; or the right of the people peaceably to assemble, and to petition the Government for a redress of grievances.

Amendment 2 - Right to Bear Arms. Ratified 12/15/1791

A well regulated Militia, being necessary to the security of a free State, the right of the people to keep and bear Arms, shall not be infringed.

Amendment 3 - Quartering of Soldiers. Ratified 12/15/1791.

No Soldier shall, in time of peace be quartered in any house, without the consent of the Owner, nor in time of war, but in a manner to be prescribed by law.

Amendment 4 - Search and Seizure. Ratified 12/15/1791.

The right of the people to be secure in their persons, houses, papers, and effects, against unreasonable searches and seizures, shall not be violated, and no Warrants shall issue, but upon probable cause, supported by Oath or affirmation, and particularly describing the place to be searched, and the persons or things to be seized.

Amendment 5 - Trial and Punishment, Compensation for Takings. Ratified 12/15/1791.

No person shall be held to answer for a capital, or otherwise infamous crime, unless on a presentment or indictment of a Grand Jury, except in cases arising in the land or naval forces, or in the Militia, when in actual service in time of War or public danger; nor shall any person be subject for the same offense to be twice put in jeopardy of life or limb; nor shall be compelled in any criminal case to be a witness against himself, nor be deprived of life, liberty, or property, without due process of law; nor shall private property be taken for public use, without just compensation.

Amendment 6 - Right to Speedy Trial, Confrontation of Witnesses. Ratified 12/15/1791.

In all criminal prosecutions, the accused shall enjoy the right to a speedy and public trial, by an impartial jury of the State and district wherein the crime shall have been committed, which district shall have been previously ascertained by law, and to be informed of the nature and cause of the accusation; to be confronted with the witnesses against him; to have compulsory process for obtaining witnesses in his favor, and to have the Assistance of Counsel for his defense.

Amendment 7 - Trial by Jury in Civil Cases. Ratified 12/15/1791.

In Suits at common law, where the value in controversy shall exceed twenty dollars, the right of trial by jury shall be preserved, and no fact tried by a jury, shall be otherwise re-examined in any Court of the United States, than according to the rules of the common law.

Amendment 8 - Cruel and Unusual Punishment. Ratified 12/15/1791.

Excessive bail shall not be required, nor excessive fines imposed, nor cruel and unusual punishments inflicted.

Amendment 9 - Construction of Constitution. Ratified 12/15/1791.

The enumeration in the Constitution, of certain rights, shall not be construed to deny or disparage others retained by the people.

Amendment 10 - Powers of the States and People. Ratified 12/15/1791.

The powers not delegated to the United States by the Constitution, nor prohibited by it to the States, are reserved to the States respectively, or to the people.

Amendment 11 - Judicial Limits. Ratified 2/7/1795.

The Judicial power of the United States shall not be construed to extend to any suit in law or equity, commenced or prosecuted against one of the United States by Citizens of another State, or by Citizens or Subjects of any Foreign State.

Amendment 12 - Choosing the President, Vice-President. Ratified 6/15/1804.

The Electors shall meet in their respective states, and vote by ballot for President and Vice-President, one of whom, at least, shall not be an inhabitant of the same state with themselves; they shall name in their ballots the person voted for as President, and in distinct ballots the person voted for as Vice-President, and they shall make distinct lists of all persons voted for as President, and of all persons voted for as Vice-President and of the number of votes for each, which lists they shall sign and certify, and transmit sealed to the seat of the government of the United States, directed to the President of the Senate;

The President of the Senate shall, in the presence of the Senate and House of Representatives, open all the certificates and the votes shall then be counted;

The person having the greatest Number of votes for President, shall be the President, if such number be a majority of the whole number of Electors appointed; and if no person have such majority, then from the persons having the highest numbers not exceeding three on the list of those voted for as President, the House of Representatives shall choose immediately, by ballot, the

President. But in choosing the President, the votes shall be taken by states, the representation from each state having one vote; a quorum for this purpose shall consist of a member or members from two-thirds of the states, and a majority of all the states shall be necessary to a choice. And if the House of Representatives shall not choose a President whenever the right of choice shall devolve upon them, before the fourth day of March next following, then the Vice-President shall act as President, as in the case of the death or other constitutional disability of the President.

The person having the greatest number of votes as Vice-President, shall be the Vice-President, if such number be a majority of the whole number of Electors appointed, and if no person have a majority, then from the two highest numbers on the list, the Senate shall choose the Vice-President; a quorum for the purpose shall consist of two-thirds of the whole number of Senators, and a majority of the whole number shall be necessary to a choice. But no person constitutionally ineligible to the office of President shall be eligible to that of Vice-President of the United States.

Amendment 13 - Slavery Abolished. Ratified 12/6/1865.

1. Neither slavery nor involuntary servitude, except as a punishment for crime whereof the party shall have been duly convicted, shall exist within the United States, or any place subject to their jurisdiction.

2. Congress shall have power to enforce this article by

appropriate legislation.

Amendment 14 - Citizenship Rights. Ratified 7/9/1868.

1. All persons born or naturalized in the United States, and subject to the jurisdiction thereof, are citizens of the United States and of the State wherein they reside. No State shall make or enforce any law which shall abridge the privileges or immunities of citizens of the United States; nor shall any State deprive any person of life, liberty, or property, without due process of law; nor deny to any person within its jurisdiction the equal protection of the laws.

2. Representatives shall be apportioned among the several States according to their respective numbers, counting the whole number of persons in each State, excluding Indians not taxed. But when the right to vote at any election for the choice of electors for President and Vice-President of the United States, Representatives in Congress, the Executive and Judicial officers of a State, or the members of the Legislature thereof, is denied to any of the male inhabitants of such State, being twenty-one years of age, and citizens of the United States, or in any way abridged, except for participation in rebellion, or other crime, the basis of representation therein shall be reduced in the proportion which the number of such male citizens shall bear to the whole number of male citizens twenty-one years of age in such State.

3. No person shall be a Senator or Representative in

Congress, or elector of President and Vice-President, or hold any office, civil or military, under the United States, or under any State, who, having previously taken an oath, as a member of Congress, or as an officer of the United States, or as a member of any State legislature, or as an executive or judicial officer of any State, to support the Constitution of the United States, shall have engaged in insurrection or rebellion against the same, or given aid or comfort to the enemies thereof. But Congress may by a vote of two-thirds of each House, remove such disability.

4. The validity of the public debt of the United States, authorized by law, including debts incurred for payment of pensions and bounties for services in suppressing insurrection or rebellion, shall not be questioned. But neither the United States nor any State shall assume or pay any debt or obligation incurred in aid of insurrection or rebellion against the United States, or any claim for the loss or emancipation of any slave; but all such debts, obligations and claims shall be held illegal and void.

5. The Congress shall have power to enforce, by appropriate legislation, the provisions of this article.

Amendment 15 - Race No Bar to Vote. Ratified 2/3/1870.

1. The right of citizens of the United States to vote shall not be denied or abridged by the United States or by any State on account of race, color, or previous condition of servitude.

2. The Congress shall have power to enforce this article by appropriate legislation.

Amendment 16 - Status of Income Tax Clarified. Ratified 2/3/1913.

The Congress shall have power to lay and collect taxes on incomes, from whatever source derived, without apportionment among the several States, and without regard to any census or enumeration.

Amendment 17 - Senators Elected by Popular Vote. Ratified 4/8/1913.

The Senate of the United States shall be composed of two Senators from each State, elected by the people thereof, for six years; and each Senator shall have one vote. The electors in each State shall have the qualifications requisite for electors of the most numerous branch of the State legislatures.

When vacancies happen in the representation of any State in the Senate, the executive authority of such State shall issue writs of election to fill such vacancies: Provided, That the legislature of any State may empower the executive thereof to make temporary appointments until the people fill the vacancies by election as the legislature may direct.

This amendment shall not be so construed as to affect the election or term of any Senator chosen before it becomes valid as part of the Constitution.

Amendment 18 - Liquor Abolished. Ratified 1/16/1919. Repealed by Amendment 21, 12/5/1933.

1. After one year from the ratification of this article the manufacture, sale, or transportation of intoxicating liquors within, the importation thereof into, or the exportation thereof from the United States and all territory subject to the jurisdiction thereof for beverage purposes is hereby prohibited.

2. The Congress and the several States shall have concurrent power to enforce this article by appropriate legislation.

3. This article shall be inoperative unless it shall have been ratified as an amendment to the Constitution by the legislatures of the several States, as provided in the Constitution, within seven years from the date of the submission hereof to the States by the Congress.

Amendment 19 - Women's Suffrage. Ratified 8/18/1920.

The right of citizens of the United States to vote shall not be denied or abridged by the United States or by any State on account of sex.

Congress shall have power to enforce this article by appropriate legislation.

Amendment 20 - Presidential, Congressional Terms. Ratified 1/23/1933.

1. The terms of the President and Vice President shall end at noon on the 20th day of January, and the terms of Senators and Representatives at noon on the 3d day of January, of the years in which such terms would have ended if this article had not been ratified; and the terms of their successors shall then begin.

2. The Congress shall assemble at least once in every year, and such meeting shall begin at noon on the 3d day of January, unless they shall by law appoint a different day.

3. If, at the time fixed for the beginning of the term of the President, the President elect shall have died, the Vice President elect shall become President. If a President shall not have been chosen before the time fixed for the beginning of his term, or if the President elect shall have failed to qualify, then the Vice President elect shall act as President until a President shall have qualified; and the Congress may by law provide for the case wherein neither a President elect nor a Vice President elect shall have qualified, declaring who shall then act as President, or the manner in which one who is to act shall be selected, and such person shall act accordingly until a President or Vice President shall have qualified.

4. The Congress may by law provide for the case of the death of any of the persons from whom the House of Representatives may choose a President whenever the right of choice shall have devolved upon them, and for the case of the death of any of the persons from whom the Senate may choose a Vice President whenever the right of choice shall have devolved upon them.

5. Sections 1 and 2 shall take effect on the 15th day of

October following the ratification of this article.

6. This article shall be inoperative unless it shall have been ratified as an amendment to the Constitution by the legislatures of three-fourths of the several States within seven years from the date of its submission.

Amendment 21 - Amendment__18 Repealed. Ratified12/5/1933.

1. The eighteenth article of amendment to the Constitution of the United States is hereby repealed.

2. The transportation or importation into any State, Territory, or possession of the United States for delivery or use therein of intoxicating liquors, in violation of the laws thereof, is hereby prohibited.

3. The article shall be inoperative unless it shall have been ratified as an amendment to the Constitution by conventions in the several States, as provided in the Constitution, within seven years from the date of the submission hereof to the States by the Congress.

Amendment 22 - Presidential Term Limits. Ratified 2/27/1951.

1. No person shall be elected to the office of the President more than twice, and no person who has held the office of President, or acted as President, for more than two years of a term to which some other person was elected President shall be elected to the office of the President more than once. But this Article shall not apply to any person holding the office of President,

when this Article was proposed by the Congress, and shall not prevent any person who may be holding the office of President, or acting as President, during the term within which this Article becomes operative from holding the office of President or acting as President during the remainder of such term.

2. This article shall be inoperative unless it shall have been ratified as an amendment to the Constitution by the legislatures of three-fourths of the several States within seven years from the date of its submission to the States by the Congress.

Amendment 23 - Presidential Vote for District of Columbia. Ratified 3/29/1961.

1. The District constituting the seat of Government of the United States shall appoint in such manner as the Congress may direct: A number of electors of President and Vice President equal to the whole number of Senators and Representatives in Congress to which the District would be entitled if it were a State, but in no event more than the least populous State; they shall be in addition to those appointed by the States, but they shall be considered, for the purposes of the election of President and Vice President, to be electors appointed by a State; and they shall meet in the District and perform such duties as provided by the twelfth article of amendment.

2. The Congress shall have power to enforce this article by appropriate legislation.

Amendment 24 - Poll Tax Barred. Ratified 1/23/1964.

1. The right of citizens of the United States to vote in any primary or other election for President or Vice President, for electors for President or Vice President, or for Senator or Representative in Congress, shall not be denied or abridged by the United States or any State by reason of failure to pay any poll tax or other tax.

2. The Congress shall have power to enforce this article by appropriate legislation.

Amendment 25 - Presidential Disability and Succession. Ratified 2/10/1967.

1. In case of the removal of the President from office or of his death or resignation, the Vice President shall become President.

2. Whenever there is a vacancy in the office of the Vice President, the President shall nominate a Vice President who shall take office upon confirmation by a majority vote of both Houses of Congress.

3. Whenever the President transmits to the President pro tempore of the Senate and the Speaker of the House of Representatives his written declaration that he is unable to discharge the powers and duties of his office, and until he transmits to them a written declaration to the contrary, such powers and duties shall be discharged by the Vice President as Acting President.

4. Whenever the Vice President and a majority of either the principal officers of the executive departments or of such other body as Congress may by law provide, transmit to the President pro tempore of the Senate and

the Speaker of the House of Representatives their written declaration that the President is unable to discharge the powers and duties of his office, the Vice President shall immediately assume the powers and duties of the office as Acting President.

Thereafter, when the President transmits to the President pro tempore of the Senate and the Speaker of the House of Representatives his written declaration that no inability exists, he shall resume the powers and duties of his office unless the Vice President and a majority of either the principal officers of the executive department or of such other body as Congress may by law provide, transmit within four days to the President pro tempore of the Senate and the Speaker of the House of Representatives their written declaration that the President is unable to discharge the powers and duties of his office. Thereupon Congress shall decide the issue, assembling within forty eight hours for that purpose if not in session. If the Congress, within twenty one days after receipt of the latter written declaration, or, if Congress is not in session, within twenty one days after Congress is required to assemble, determines by two thirds vote of both Houses that the President is unable to discharge the powers and duties of his office, the Vice President shall continue to discharge the same as Acting President; otherwise, the President shall resume the powers and duties of his office.

Amendment 26 - Voting Age Set to 18 Years. Ratified 7/1/1971.

1. The right of citizens of the United States, who are

eighteen years of age or older, to vote shall not be denied or abridged by the United States or by any State on account of age.

2. The Congress shall have power to enforce this article by appropriate legislation.

Amendment 27 - Limiting Changes to Congressional Pay. Ratified 5/7/1992.

No law, varying the compensation for the services of the Senators and Representatives, shall take effect, until an election of Representatives shall have intervened.

Bibliography

Alexander, John K. *Samuel Adams: America's Revolutionary Politician.* Rowman and Littlefield, 2002.

Bailyn, Bernard. "The Ideological Origins of the American Revolution." Cambridge, Massachusetts: The Belknap Press of Harvard University Press, 1992.

Berger, Raoul. *Government by Judiciary.* 2nd. Indianapolis, Indiana: Liberty Fund, 1997.

Bradford, M.E. *Original Intentions: On The Making and Ratification Of The United States Constitution.* Athens, Georgia: The University of Georgi Press, 1993.

Burgh, James. *Political Disquisitions.* Reproduction from British Library. Vol. 1. 3 vols. London: Gale ECCO, 2010.

Colburn, Trevor. "The Lamp of Experience." In *Whig History and the Intellectual Origins of the American Revolution*, by Trevor Colbourn. Indianapolis, Indiana: Liberty Fund, Inc., 1998.

Conley, Patrick T., ed. *The Constitution And The States.* Madison, Wisconsin: Madison House, 1988.

Davis, Jefferson. *The Rise and Fall of The Confederate Government.* Vol. I. II vols. New York: De Capo Press, 1990.

"Democracy, Liberty, and Property." In *The State Constitutional Conventions of the 1820's*, edited by Merill D. Peterson. Indianapolis, Indiana: Liberty Fund, Inc., 2010.

Elliot, Jonathan, ed. *Elliots Debates on the Federal Constitution.* Vol. I. V vols. Philidelphia, Pennsylvania: J. B. Lippincott & Co., 1859.

Farrand, Max, ed. *The Records of the Federal Convention of 1787 v.I.* Vol. I. IV vols. New Haven & London: Yale University Press, 1966.

Farrand, Max, ed. *The Records of the Federal Convention of 1787 v.III.* Vol. III. IV vols. Westford, Massachusetts: Yale University Press, 1966.

Fleming, Walter Lynwood. "The South in the Building of the Nation." *The History of Southern States.* Digitized. Vol. I. Edited by Julian Alvin Carrol Chandler. Richmond, Virginia: The Southern Historical Publication Society, 1909.

Gutzman, Kevin R.C. *Virginia's American Revolution.* Lanham, Maryland: Lexington Books, 2007.

History.org, Teaching American. *Farewell Speech.* May 12, 2011. http://teachingamericanhistory.org/library/index.asp?document=491 (accessed May 12, 2011).

Hutson, James H., ed. *Supplement to Max Farrand's The Records of the Federal Convention of 1787.* New Haven & London: Yale University Press, 1987.

Jefferson, Thomas. *The Portable Thomas Jefferson.* Electronic Book. Edited by Merrill D. Peterson. New York: Penquin Books, 1975.

Jensen, Merrill. *The Articles of Confederation.* Madison, Wisconsin: The University of Wisconsin Press, 1976.

Jensen, Merrill, ed. *The Documentary History Of The Ratification Of The Constitution Volume II.* Vol. II. Madison, Wisconsin: State Historical Society of Wisconsin, 1976.

Kaminski, Johm P., ed. *The Documetary History Of The Ratification Of The Constitution XVI.* Vol. 4. Madison,

Wisconsin: State Historical Society of Wisconsin, 1986.

Kaminski, John P., ed. *The Documentary History of The Ratification Of The Constitution.* Vol. XIX. Madison, Wisconsin: Wisconsin Historical Society Press, 2003.

Kaminski, John P., ed. *The Documentary History of the Ratification of the Constitution VI.* Vol. VI. Madsion: State Historical Society of Wisconsin, 2000.

Kaminski, John P., ed. *The Documentary History of The Ratification of The Constitution: New York.* Vol. XXIII. Madsion, Wisconsin: Wisconsin Historical Society Press, 2009.

Kaminski, John P., ed. *The Documentary History Of The Ratification of The Constitution: New York.* Vol. XX. Madsion, Wisconsin: Wisconsin Historical Society Press, 2004.

Kaminski, John P., ed. *The Documentary History of The Ratification of The Constitution:Virginia.* Vol. X. Madison, Wisconsin: State Historical Society of Wisconsin, 1993.

Kaminski, John P., ed. *The Documentary History Of The Ratifiication Of The Constitution XIII.* Vol. I. Madison, Wisconsin: State Historical Society of Wisconsin, 1981.

Klein, Milton M., ed. *The Empire State: A History of New York.* Ithaca and London: Cornell University Press, 2001.

Lewis, Paul. *The Grand Incendiary.* New York: The Dial Press, 1973.

Library, Lillian Goldman Law. *British-American Diplomacy.* 2008.   http://avalon.law.yale.edu/18th_century/paris.asp (accessed September 20, 2010).

Locke, John. *Two Treatises of Government.* Cambridge Texts in the History of Political Thought: Student Edition. Edited by Peter Laslett. London: Cambridge University Press, 1698.

Lutz, Donald S. "Colonial Origins of the American Constitution." In *A Documentary History*, edited by Donald S. Lutz. Indianapolis, Indiana: The Liberty Fund, 1998.

Maier, Pauline. *Ratification: The People Debate the Constitution, 1787-1788.* New York, New York: Simon & Schuster, 2010.

Martin, Luther. *Sercret Proceedings and Debates of the Constitutional Convention 1787.* Reprinted from 1986 Edition. Honolulu, Hawaii: University Press of The Pacific, 2002.

Mayer, David N. *The Constitutional Thought of Thomas Jefferson.* University of Virginia Press, 1994.

Mc Donald, Forrest. *E Pluribus Unum: The Formation of The American Republic 1776-1790.* 2nd. Indianapolis: Liberty Fund, 1979.

Mc Donald, Forrest. "States Rights And The Union 1776-1876." In *Imperium in Imperia*. Lawrence, Kansas: University Press of Kansas, 2000.

McClellan, James. *Liberty, Order, and Justice: An Introduction to the Constitutional Principles of American Government*. 3rd. Indianapolis: Liberty Fund, 2000.

Morris, Richard B. "The Albany Congress: Its Role in American Constitutional History." *Program of the Board of Regents of The University of the State of New York Commemorating the 200th Anniversary of the Albany Plan of Union.* Albany, New York, 1954. 15.

Newbold, Robert C. "The Albany Congress and Plan of Union of 1754." New York: Vantage Press, 1955.

Press, Associated. *Fox News.com.* April 15, 2009. http://www.foxnews.com/politics/2009/04/15/governor-says-texans-want-secede-union-probably-wont/ (accessed September 20, 2010).

Ratification of the Constitution by the State of North Carolina. May 3, 2011. http://www.constitution.org/rc/rat_decl-nc.htm (accessed May Wednesday, 2011).

Sidney, Algernon. *Discourses Concerning Government.* Revised Edition. Edited by Thomas G. West. Indianapolis: Liberty Fund, 1996.

Society, Constitution. *The Kentucky Resolutions of 1798.* http://www.constitution.org/cons/kent1798.htm (accessed 5 9, 2011).

South Carolina Ordinance of Nullification, November 24, 1832. May 11, 2011. http://avalon.law.yale.edu/19th_century/ordnull.asp (accessed May 11, 2011).

Spaulding, E. Wilder. *New York in The Critical Period: 1783-1789.* New York, New York: Columbia University Press, 1932.

Stephens, Alexander. *A Constitutional View of the late War Between The States.* Vol. I. II vols. Harrisburg, Virginia: Sprinkle Publications, 1994.

Stoll, Ira. *Samuel Adams: A Life.* New York: Free Press, 2008.

Taylor, John. *Construction Construed and Constitutions*

Vindicated. Reprint of the 1820 Edition. Clark, New Jersey: The LawBook Exchange, 2009.

Taylor, John. "New Views of The Constitution." In *New Views of The Constitution of The United States*. Washington, D.C.: The Lawbook Exchange, LTD., 1823.

Trenchard, John. *Cato's Letters*. Edited by Ronald Hamowy. Vol. 1. 2 vols. Indianapolis: Liberty Fund, 1995.

Tucker, St. George. *View of the Constitution of the United States with Selected Writings*. Indianapolis, Indiana: Liberty Fund, 1999.

Tyner, Jarvis. *Hope is stronger than hate.* September 30, 2010.   http://www.cpusa.org/hope-is-stronger-than-hate/ (accessed October 30, 2010).

Weisberg, Jacob. *A Tea Party Taxonomy.* September 18, 2010. http://www.newsweek.com/2010/09/18/the-tea-party-s-anarchist-streak.html (accessed October 30, 2010).

Wills, Gary. *Lincoln at Gettysburg.* New York, New York: Simon and Schuster, 1992.

About The Author

Rick M. Montes is a New York State Coordinator for the Tenth Amendment Center, a national think tank that works to preserve and protect the principles of strictly limited government through information, education, and activism.

He holds a B.A. in Legal Studies, graduating Magna Cum Laude from the State University of New York, College at Purchase and is currently finishing his M.A. in History at Western Connecticut State University.

15501765R00063

Made in the USA
Lexington, KY
12 November 2018